INSTANT REPEAT BUSINESS

Other Books in the Instant Success Series

Successful Franchising by Bradley J. Sugars
The Real Estate Coach by Bradley J. Sugars
Billionaire in Training by Bradley J. Sugars
Instant Cashflow by Bradley J. Sugars
Instant Sales by Bradley J. Sugars
Instant Leads by Bradley J. Sugars
Instant Profit by Bradley J. Sugars
Instant Promotions by Bradley J. Sugars
Instant Team Building by Bradley J. Sugars
Instant Systems by Bradley J. Sugars
Instant Referrals by Bradley J. Sugars
Instant Advertising by Bradley J. Sugars
The Business Coach by Bradley J. Sugars

INSTANT REPEAT BUSINESS

BRADLEY J. SUGARS

McGraw-Hill
New York Chicago San Francisco Lisbon London
Madrid Mexico City Milan New Delhi San Juan
Seoul Singapore Sydney Toronto

The McGraw-Hill Companies

2 3 4 5 6 7 8 9 0 FGR/FGR 0 9 8 7 6

ISBN 0-07-146666-5

McGraw-Hill books are available at special quantity discounts to use as premiums and sales promotions, or for use in corporate training programs. For more information, please write to the Director of Special Sales, McGraw-Hill Professional, Two Penn Plaza, New York, NY 10121-2298. Or contact your local bookstore.

Library of Congress Cataloging-in-Publication Data

Sugars, Bradley J.
Instant repeat business / Bradley J. Sugars.
p. cm.
ISBN 0-07-146666-5 (alk. paper)
1. Customer services. 2. Consumer satisfaction. I. Title.
HF5415.5.S84 2006
658.8'12—dc22 2005025418

Dedicated to all *Action* Business Coaches, leaders in every sense of the word.

CONTENTS

INTRODUCTION

Hanging on to an existing customer is far easier, and much cheaper, than looking for a new one. It never ceases to amaze me how few businesses realize this. They seem to have it ingrained in their thinking that the business cycle must remain sharply focused on continually hunting for new customers. They allocate large sums of money to advertising and marketing, trusting this will lure prospects from the opposition or entice others to buy products they really hadn't thought about or had a need for.

Take a look around and observe the way the vast majority of businesses conduct themselves. Notice the thrust of their activities. Become sensitive to the messages they're putting out.

What should strike you is their relentless effort to fish for new business. They seem infatuated with appealing to a fresh group of potential customers. They seem obsessed with appealing to people who have never dealt with them before.

But what about their existing customers? Have they been forgotten, or is it just assumed that once a person becomes a customer, they'll remain a customer? Most pay very little attention to keeping close to their existing customers at all. In fact, most would have no idea who their existing customers are and how to make contact with them.

I have eaten at many restaurants in my time, and I'm not on any databases. I've never received a letter from any of them asking me to dine there again. Yet I know these restaurants spend large sums on advertising and marketing efforts like offering discounted meals to new patrons. How much easier, and cheaper, would it be to look after existing patrons? They'd be able to comfortably predict future ordering requirements, not to mention cashflow, if they pandered to an existing, loyal, customer base. You see, happy customers are always willing to return because they feel comfortable with the entire setup—the product, the atmosphere, the staff, and the pricing. People like to avoid the unknown as much as possible and don't like taking chances, especially when they're paying for it.

How do you ensure that those customers you already have make repeat purchases? How do you get them to buy more from you? Useful techniques will be outlined in this book. You'll learn the secrets to ensuring that your customers feel so special they'll do your selling for you!

This book is all about looking after repeat business. It's all about ensuring that your existing client base remains happy, loyal, and content with your business. It's all about ensuring that you look after that 20 percent of your customer base that accounts for 80 percent of your revenue. It's all about turning your existing customers into your most prized asset—Raving Fans.

To make sure you understand clearly where repeat business fits into your business cycle, I'm going to briefly mention a very important concept. This is the concept I call The Business Chassis. Read more about this in my book *Instant Cashflow.*

The Business Chassis looks like this:

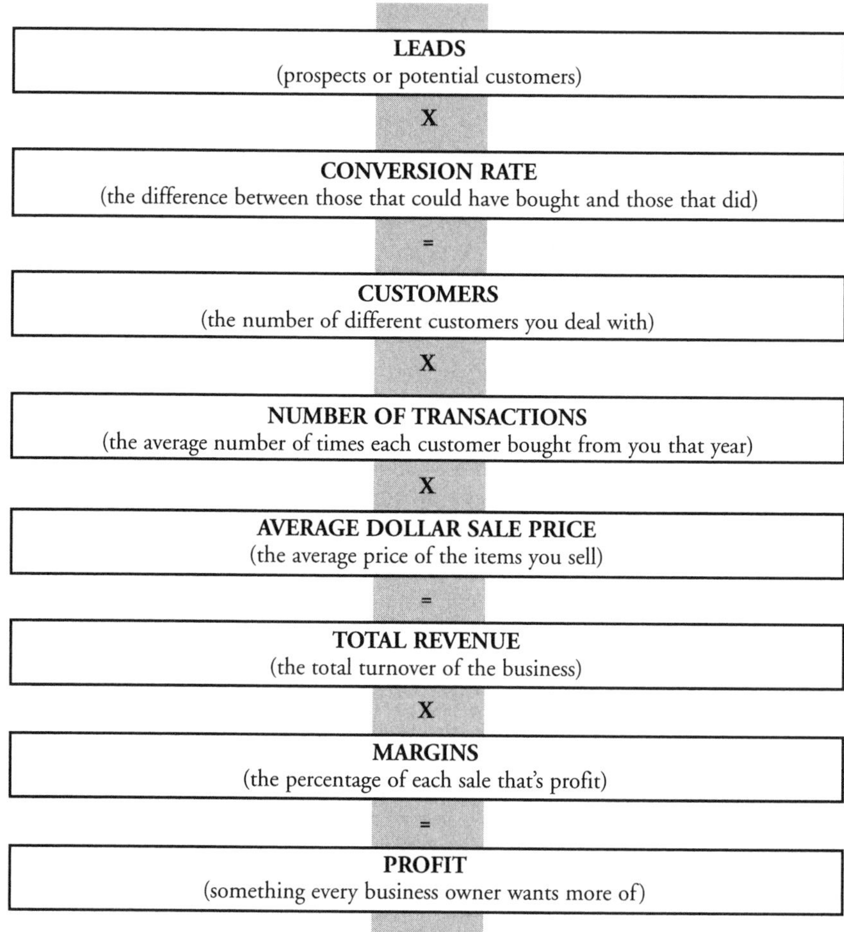

LEADS
(prospects or potential customers)
X
CONVERSION RATE
(the difference between those that could have bought and those that did)
=
CUSTOMERS
(the number of different customers you deal with)
X
NUMBER OF TRANSACTIONS
(the average number of times each customer bought from you that year)
X
AVERAGE DOLLAR SALE PRICE
(the average price of the items you sell)
=
TOTAL REVENUE
(the total turnover of the business)
X
MARGINS
(the percentage of each sale that's profit)
=
PROFIT
(something every business owner wants more of)

As you can see, repeat business has to do with that part of the Business Chassis called Number of Transactions. The process began when you decided to generate leads (read my books *Instant Leads* and *Instant Promotions* for more in-depth information about this) and ended up with some prospects. These you converted into customers by selling to them (read my book *Instant Sales* for more on this). Your task now is to ensure that they continue doing business with you.

So, congratulations on deciding to take proactive steps to growing your business. By concentrating on first things first, you'll set in motion a chain of activities that will generate more business for you by increasing your number of transactions. I personally guarantee it.

How to Use This Book

This book is divided into different parts, one for each of the major areas I'll be discussing.

Pick the part that interests you most, jump right in, and begin working through the steps outlined. You see, there are things you must give careful consideration to before getting carried away doing the "fun" things involved in chasing repeat business.

You'll notice repetition in many of the steps outlined. This is because this book outlines, in practical terms, how to go about improving the number of transactions your business currently enjoys from each customer.

You might decide to implement all the great ideas explained in this book all at once. Or you might decide to implement them one at a time. But whatever you decide, the important thing is you'll no longer be blundering around in the dark, unsure whether what you're doing has a chance of increasing the number of times each customer buys from you, or not.

We'll visit Charlie, my trusted mechanic, and catch up with him as he devises strategies to get his customers to do business with him more often. You see, he had come to realize his mechanical workshop was, in reality, only providing him with a job. He realized he was working harder as a small business owner than he did when he worked as a mechanic for someone else. Sure, he's great at what he does and I swear by him. But at the end of the day his business was going nowhere.

He called me in and asked for help. He wanted me to coach him to business success. This I agreed to do, and so began a Mentoring Program aimed at turning his business around. He was apprehensive at first, feeling more like a fish out of water than a mechanic doing his best to grow his business. But he soon got over that as he discovered marketing could be *fun*. He began to realize that it was something anybody could do well if they tried. The mystique of marketing soon began to disappear as we worked our way through some of the concepts and strategies selected for his business.

Sit in on this next coaching session as we delve into the age-old question of getting people to do business with you more often.

You might also be surprised at how much this exercise will reveal about your business. It may get you thinking about important issues that have never crossed your mind before. If some of this information is new to you, don't be concerned—there's never been a better time to start improving the way you run your business.

Make sure you make notes as you go along. When you come to deciding what you're going to do to improve your bottom line, you'll find it useful referring back to them. You'll find proven examples and ideas that, when combined with your new knowledge, will bring results.

Now it's time to get started. There are customers out there waiting to deal with you.

Charlie's Repeat Business Roller Coaster

I knew Charlie was looking forward to this session. Getting customers to remain customers seemed to be the one area he was having difficulty in. He told me he found this strange, as he knew the quality of his workmanship was high and his customers always seemed more than satisfied.

I, too, was looking forward to showing him how he could chase repeat business. He was now very used to thinking like a business owner and not a mechanic, or a worker for that matter. I helped him see he needed to ensure he didn't end up an employee in his own business, and that's exactly the way he was heading. He was spending far too much time working *in* the business and not *on* it, and that had to change.

"Good morning, Charlie," I said as I entered his small office and looked through the window into the busy workshop. I habitually did that just to see what delights he had in at the time.

"I haven't seen that Maserati before," I said. "New customer?"

"Yeah, phoned in after my last ad. And he wasn't the only one, Brad. I received 15 calls and of those, 5 have either made appointments for a service or have already been in. Not bad, huh?"

"That's terrific, Charlie. That's a 30 percent conversion rate."

"Yes, I know. But what I'm really looking forward to now is increasing their number of transactions."

"You've come a long way, Charlie. You're already talking like a businessman! In fact, you're doing better than that—you're *thinking* like a businessman."

"It's just like you said, Brad. If I can do it, anyone can."

As always, I was going to start the session off by going back to basics. It never hurts to go over some of the ground rules and fundamental concepts.

"As you know, to be classified as a customer, your prospect needs to have spent money, and you need to have recorded the sale in your database. This last step may seem strange, but it is most important because it allows you to differentiate on your database between prospects and customers. You see, if you are planning to send a letter out to all prospects offering them an incentive to come and have work done for the first time, you don't want to be sending it to people who are already customers. This record will also tell you when they last were in, how often they service their cars, and what their average dollar sale is."

Charlie sat riveted, nodding every now and then as I spoke. I pressed on.

"Here's something you'll find interesting, Charlie. I find most businesses put up a huge *stop* sign at this level. Businesses seem to sit back waiting for these customers to return, instead of being proactive and inviting them back. Understand at the customer level, they have cost you money. If you are content to stop at this level, your business will eventually go broke. I have eaten out at many restaurants, and guess what? I'm not on any database. I've never received a letter from any of them saying: 'Brad, we'd love to have you back.' This is, to my mind, quite insane. They seem to be saying, 'You've bought, now I'm going to just hope like heck you come back.' Think about the possibilities for your business, Charlie. The *stop* sign is the scariest thing I've come across in business. You need to get rid of it, and fast."

"You scare me, Brad. I hadn't thought of it that way before. But please go on—I don't mean to stop you."

"What I want you to aim towards is developing a loyal group of customers. I want you to turn your customers into what I call Raving Fans. These are people who can't stop selling for you—you know, telling all their friends to come here too. They're your greatest asset, believe me. So, when your customers bring their cars in for their second service, or make their second purchase, they become what I call 'Members' of your business. They now have a feeling of belonging. And being a Member is a step up the ladder of loyalty that has Raving Fans at the top rung. Understand?"

"Yes, I think so. But what comes after Member, then? Are there other steps before Raving Fan?"

"Only one, Charlie. And that's Advocate. Advocates are people who sell you to other people—they give referrals or promote you to others. The big difference between Advocates and Raving Fans is the Raving Fans are Advocates who can't stop selling for you. They're rather like another member of your team. Get it?"

Charlie nodded.

"So you see, once you have converted prospects to customers by doing business with them, you move them up the ladder of loyalty by doing business with them more than once—How easy is that, by the way? Then, it's a simple thing to get them to become Advocates by giving them great service and all the other things we're going to talk about today. From there they'll quickly become Raving Fans when the *wow* factor kicks in."

"The what?"

"The *wow* factor. Understand this: the fundamentals of creating great customer service involve creating a system to make sure your customers' expectations are surpassed every time. Having satisfied customers implies you have given them all they've wanted, but nothing more. But if you're going to surpass their expectations, you must systematically go beyond their expectations. Every single day you need to be getting better. The Japanese have a good term for this. They call it *Kaizen*, which means constant and never-ending improvement."

"You're blowing me away, Brad. Yet it all sounds so logical, doesn't it?"

"That's the point, Charlie. It is. And that's what makes it so powerful. That's what makes it so achievable."

Charlie was agreeing with everything I said.

"You see, customers who make two purchases are 10 times more likely to make more than someone who has only made one. So you need to put some effort into your members. Give them a membership card and a membership pack. How many of your customers know all your products or everything you can do for their cars? Very few, I would suggest. So why not include a catalog or brochure in the membership pack? You can also include samples, vouchers, and things like that. One interesting example I came across recently was at a truck stop in New Zealand. The owner pinned up photographs on a notice board of all drivers who had stopped the night there. Then there's the coffee shop that gives you your own personalized coffee mug. Each time you come in, they get your mug down from the shelf for you. These two examples give members a sense of belonging."

"That's fascinating, Brad. I never thought of running my business like that before. But I sure can see how it'll benefit me."

"Increasing the number of transactions your customers make is working on the third part of the Business Chassis, Charlie. Remember the Business Chassis we spoke about before?"

He nodded.

"Good. And remember what I said about it? Working on the Chassis' five main elements is the *only* way to increase the profits of your business. You've already put strategies in place to increase the number of leads you get (read more about this in my books *Instant Leads* and *Instant Promotions*), and you've addressed increasing your conversion rate (read more about this in my book *Instant Sales*), so now it's time to consider ways of increasing your number of transactions. Is that OK?"

"Fine by me, Brad. Where do we start?"

"We're going to start by looking at creating your very own newsletter. And not just any old newsletter, but one that gets read and results in repeat business. We're going to look at closed-door sales, and loyalty strategies. These strategies are sure to pump up your business by ensuring you get the sort of repeat business that'll make your competitors green with envy."

"Great, Brad, let's do it."

INSTANT REPEAT BUSINESS

Part 1

I Newsletters

"It's time to now look at newsletters as a tool to generate repeat business, Charlie. Have you ever thought about producing your own?"

"No, Brad, that's way too involved for a small business like this. Besides, I just don't have the expertise, or the budget, to consider them."

"Let me put it this way. Do your competitors have newsletters?"

"Quite a few, Brad. There's the quick fitment center around the corner. They're a franchise, so they get one whether they want one or not. Then there's the exhaust shop that produces a black-and-white newsletter each quarter. It's not much, I must admit. It's cheaply produced on their photocopy machine, I'd say. I don't know about the other mechanical workshops, though."

"So they're fairly well accepted in the industry then, by the sounds of it. The trick, of course, is to have one that gets read and acted upon. You see, the whole objective here is to get your cash register ringing."

"That's all very well and good, but they still take a lot of know-how to produce, don't they? I mean, I'm no journalist, and I'm not about to hire one, if you know what I mean."

"You're right and wrong, Charlie. Yes, they do involve some know-how, and that's what I'm about to give you. And no, you certainly don't have to be a journalist to produce one. In fact, you don't need great writing skills at all. But we'll get to that in a moment."

Charlie looked unconvinced.

"I think I'm about to reach my level of incompetence, Brad. I feel I'm pushing the boundaries of my business ability here."

"Let me explain it this way, Charlie. Newsletters are certainly a lot more sophisticated or complicated than the tools we've discussed so far, but that doesn't mean *you* can't make excellent use of them. It also doesn't mean you can't do them well yourself. You see, I'm going to show you how to produce a professional-looking newsletter that will amaze your customers. They'll think you're in a different league than your competition. It'll reflect well on your business because it'll send out a quality image. It will set you up as an expert in your field and it won't be a huge drain on your resources, including your time. Unconvinced? Well, let me explain by starting at the beginning."

What Is a Successful Newsletter?

Basically any newsletter that is widely read, and results in increased sales, can be considered successful. The objective of your newsletter is not to bore people with uninteresting articles where you just talk about yourself; the objective is to remind them of who you are, and to get them to buy from you again.

As you probably know, to get a new customer you need to invest money in marketing. This means you have an acquisition cost for each new customer. Your acquisition cost is determined by how much your marketing costs you, divided by how many customers it brings into your store.

Once you've calculated this figure, you can then work out how many times each customer needs to purchase from you before she becomes profitable. In the average business this will mean selling to her two times before you begin to make a profit.

Your newsletter, then, is the tool you use to ensure your past customers come back on a regular basis. If they buy from you only once, you're actually losing money each time you acquire a new one. By using a well-formatted newsletter, you increase the number of times they do business with you, thus turning them into profitable customers.

What Makes a Successful Newsletter?

There are a number of key elements which, when combined, go into making up a successful newsletter. The most important of these is the content. You'll find out which article types work best shortly. Another important consideration is any offers you're making. No matter how well written, or entertaining, your newsletter is, if you don't make great offers, it will not bring you additional sales.

In the following pages, you'll learn how to write newsletter headlines that work, how to position your photographs for maximum impact, and which typefaces have the best recognition rates. You'll discover which stock your newsletter should be printed on, what size it should be, and which articles, angles, and appeals work best.

The Seven Steps to Newsletter Success

Step 1: Who Is Your Target Market?

If you don't know who your target market is, it's almost impossible to attract them. Remember what I said about trying to get a date without knowing which gender you're interested in? Remember, the "let's see" method of marketing tends to fail every time.

So let's get specific. Who are the people most likely to be interested in your product or service? Here are some guidelines:

Age: How old are they? Don't just say "all ages" or "a variety." Think of an age that symbolizes most of them.

Sex: Are they male or female? "Half and half" is too broad.

Income: How much do they make?

Where do they live?: Are they local, or do they come from miles around to deal with you?

What are their interests?: If you don't know what they're interested in, how can you design a newsletter that will capture their attention?

Step 2: Where Do You Send Your Newsletter?

Ask most businesses where they send their newsletters and you'll get the same response—to past customers. Of course, this is exactly who you want to send your newsletters to, but aren't you forgetting someone?

Unconverted prospects should also be added to your newsletter mailing list. The reason for this is quite simple. The fact that they didn't buy from you the first time doesn't mean they won't buy from you in the future. You invested money in getting them to visit you in the first place, so why not invest a little more in getting them to come back?

There can be a variety of reasons why people didn't buy from you initially. Perhaps you didn't have the exact model they were after, or maybe they weren't in a position to buy at that time. By keeping in contact with them, you give yourself the chance of doing business with them in the future.

Even if they have bought from someone else, you might be able to pick up some business from them for their parts and accessories requirements.

When you really think about it, the more people who read your newsletter, the more sales you'll make from it. All you need to make your newsletter a success is a database of prospects to mail it to.

There are basically three ways to acquire a mailing list:

Buy one from a broker. This is a quick, but expensive, way to get a mailing list. Remember that the idea of having a newsletter is to keep in contact with people who have already dealt with your business in the past? Sending your newsletter to a "cold list" is not as effective as mailing to someone who already knows who you are.

Mail to someone else's list. Find a noncompetitive company with a similar target market to your own. Then simply ask them if you could mail to their list or include your newsletter with one of their upcoming mailouts. Once again, this method is not as effective as dealing with people who are familiar with your business.

Create your own. This is one of the fastest and most effective ways to put together a list of people who are interested in your product or service. The quickest way to compile your own list is to run a competition. To enter, people simply need to write their name and address on the entry form provided and then drop it into a box or mail it in.

Of course, you can always just ask people if they'd like to receive your newsletter on a regular basis. Most people will probably say yes. You can then either have them fill out a form with their name and address, or take their details from your accounts.

Step 3: What Do You Want to Say?

We'll cover the content of your newsletter in more depth shortly, but for the moment we need to look at what it is you want from people reading your newsletter.

Although a newsletter has the benefit of keeping your name in your customer's mind, at the end of the day it needs to bring you more business. So understanding that we want to make sales, and get increased revenue, we need to look at the style in which we write our newsletter.

People will only read newsletters that contain interesting articles. They will not read a newsletter that is just one big sales pitch. The challenge is that we want to make sales from it. So how do we sell without looking like we're trying to sell?

Quite simply, we need to do both. People will tolerate some selling messages, providing there is enough nonselling content to make it worth their while reading on. But it is possible to sell without looking like that's what you're trying to do.

The easiest way to do this is by featuring articles on new products or services that you offer. By discussing the benefits of these products throughout the article, you can get readers ready to buy. All you need to do then is point out at the end of the article that you stock the product or provide that service.

People will be knocking you over in the rush to buy what you're trying to sell.

Another way is to simply position yourself as the expert on a particular product or service. Discuss how the product works and what to look for when buying it. Customers will begin to view you as the expert and will come to you seeking further advice. Of course your advice will be to buy the particular model you just happen to have in stock.

The main thing you need to remember when writing your newsletter is that you need to say something to your potential readers. There must be a subtle message you are conveying. This may be in the form of an offer you want to make, an important point of difference, a list of the benefits of dealing with you, or something newsworthy about your product or service.

It's essential that *what* you say is appealing to *whom* you are trying to say it to. For example, writing favorable articles about the sex industry in a newsletter aimed at old people probably won't work. Articles that look at historical events probably would.

Let's deal now with each type of message, one by one.

Strong Offer

This is the most commonly used, and the one that tends to work the best. Remember that people are totally uninterested in reading a newsletter that does nothing but "sell." They've usually picked up the publication to keep informed and to be entertained. But you still need to sell in your newsletter, so make sure that you put a strong offer somewhere in it. Make sure the offer you give them is worthwhile, the type that will have your phone ringing off the hook. I'll discuss this in more detail later.

Point of Difference

This can work well when there is a large market for your product and you have many competitors. For example, if you're writing a newsletter for a clothing store, you may find it hard to convince people they should be coming to you and you only. But if you discussed the fact that yours is the only store that offers exclusive, after-hours showings along with a free glass of wine and snacks, then people will be sold on the idea of dealing with you.

Listing the Benefits

If you don't have a strong offer or point of difference, listing the benefits of dealing with you may do the trick. For example, a hairdresser could list the four reasons she gives the best haircuts in town, or a beauty salon could emphasize the six ways a prospect's skin will improve after one visit.

Most importantly, you must relate the benefits to the customer. Remember, always write your newsletter with their favorite subject in mind—*them.*

If you want to demonstrate the ways your business is superior to the competition, one of the more discrete ways of doing this is to write a section on the things to look out for. Those things that should be avoided. This is the most credible way to attack your opposition. But always remember that you can't name names.

Something Newsworthy

Perhaps you've just opened a new room in your restaurant, or you have a famous author coming in for book signings. Maybe you've just been given an award, or one of your staff has done something amazing for a customer. If something has happened that has genuine interest, tell your readers about it.

Step 4: How to Write Your Newsletter

Now that we've covered the basics, it's time to get into the nuts and bolts of how to construct your newsletter.

First you're going to need a name for your newsletter. Take a bit of time to think about this one, as the right name can make a huge difference. There are basically two ways to approach it—a humorous name or a serious name.

A funny name can really get the ball rolling, especially if it's a clever play on words. A good example of an effective word play would be a men's clothing store with a newsletter called The Well-Dressed Mail, or a fencing company calling their newsletter the Steel & Wooden Post.

Be careful when choosing a humorous name. If yours is the type of business that deals with serious problems or conservative clients, it wouldn't do to have an amusing newsletter title. Can you imagine the type of negative reaction you'd get if you owned a hair loss center and had a newsletter called The Bald Bulletin? Sometimes you're better off to play on the safe side.

There's another obvious but often forgotten item that needs to be included is your contact details. I've seen it happen many times before where people simply forget to include the business address and phone number. Now some people may argue that their customers already know where they are, and would probably have their phone number already. But what if the newsletter were passed on to a friend? Besides, you need to make it easy for people if you want them to take action. If they have to go to a lot of effort just to find your phone number, they'll more often than not just give up. So include all relevant information including e-mail addresses or Web sites.

If you have a Web site that you regularly update, it's well worthwhile advertising the fact in your newsletter. This will give it the exposure it needs so that it can start making you money.

So let's take a look at the other sections and inclusions that will make your newsletter a success.

USP and Guarantee

Two things that you should consider including in your newsletter are your Unique Selling Proposition (USP) and any guarantees you offer. Your USP is the one thing that is truly different about you, or at least the one thing you can promote as being different.

A successful USP should be:

- Truly unique.
- Exciting to your target market.
- Something that will have your customers telling their friends about it.
- Something that can't be easily copied.

A lot of business owners wonder why they need a uniqueness at all. Shouldn't there be room for dozens of "me-too" businesses? The fact is, there isn't, and the "me-too" businesses will ultimately go to the wall.

If you don't have an existing USP, you'll need to find one. Start by listing everything you do that could be considered even a little bit unique. These points don't have to be earth shattering; they just need to be different enough to stand out.

To get you started, here's a list of some possible USPs you could adopt:

- You sell a higher quality product or service, and you can specifically show how it benefits the customer in a meaningful way.
- You provide better customer service and you can easily explain and promote why you're better.
- You offer a better or longer guarantee and you have it written down.
- You offer more choice/selection/options, and this is something people want and always look for.

- You offer a trade-in program and no one else does.
- You serve a specific (yet sizable) demographic group that is overlooked by most competitors.
- You offer a better or more generous bonus points or loyalty club system and your product or service is at least as good.
- You have the best after-sales service, and this is something you can explain to people easily when they buy.
- Your product or service has unique features people care about.
- You offer attractive products or services no one else does.
- You have a "special ingredient."
- You install and deliver for free.

These are just a few examples of unique, salable points. If you think hard enough about it, you're sure to find something you are currently doing that is unique. It's also possible you'll discover something you *should* be doing that would make you unique.

Basically, your uniqueness comes from one of seven areas: quality, price, service, delivery, speed, convenience, and experience. Regardless of what it is, you need to promote it at every available opportunity, and there's no better place to start than with your newsletter.

Your Very Own Newspaper

One of the things many people don't consider when they're producing their own newsletter is that it really is their very own newspaper. Now it's obviously not going to be considered a daily paper, nor even a weekly or monthly publication. But the rules for producing your newsletter are the same as those for a paper.

For starters, your newsletter should have an exciting lead story. Now it's not going to be about politics or scandal, but it does need to generate interest. This is important because if you don't get people interested in what you've got to say with your very first story, you won't get them reading on.

Now there are many ways to get off to a fast start, article-wise. Look through the stories you want to run with for each issue, take the one you think most people will be interested in, and lead with that. Hit them straight up with a powerful, curiosity-provoking headline, and keep them going from there.

Remember that while your newsletter has some distinct similarities to a newspaper, you should only ever talk about things that are relevant to your business, or of interest to your readers. Don't try to report on things that have no relevance. Always remember that the main aim of your newsletter is to make sales.

Product Previews and Reviews

This is easily the second most exciting section you can include in any newsletter. In case you're wondering what the most exciting is, don't worry; we'll get to that shortly.

People who are interested in your products or services will always be interested in finding out about new products, or in the case of a service-based business, new techniques. So, therefore, previewing new products will ensure a high readership.

There are two basic ways to go about it.

The first is to simply look at the features, and more importantly, the benefits of new products as they come onto the market. In many cases you can get editorial style material from the suppliers themselves. Major suppliers will probably have paid an advertising agency, or public relations company, to write something for them about their new products.

Remember, there's no point talking about a product you don't have, or can't get. If your article is designed to get people excited (and it should be), you need to get them coming into your store to purchase, and not shopping around somewhere else.

This raises another important point. What if your price is higher than that of your opposition?

By doing an in-depth review of the product or technique, you position yourself as the expert and therefore justify the extra expenditure. A particularly effective technique is to talk about the need for top-quality advice before people make the purchase decision. For example, maybe you need to have your hand measured professionally to ensure the correct size before you have new grips fitted to your golf clubs. Or perhaps the buyer will need to be instructed on how to use a particular piece of machinery to avoid damaging it.

The point is this; you're now giving your customers a reason why they need to come to see *you*.

The second way to write up a new product is by doing a comparison or "test run" against other new products on the market. Car magazines often do this when they run "showdowns" between new models competing for the same market placement.

This technique gives you the chance to compare your product in a favorable light to those stocked by your opposition. You can show how your product outperforms those produced by other companies. But a word of warning: you need to ensure your tests are objective and not simply designed to run down the opposition's product.

You can't expect people to believe what you're saying if you're blatantly attacking another firm's product. You also need to clearly explain that you have run these tests, and any conclusions you've gained are purely your opinion. This is important from a legal standpoint, as you'll most likely not be running your tests under scientific conditions and with an unbiased, independent party supervising your trial.

It's always a good idea when doing these comparisons to have a picture of your product beside a summary table where a direct comparison can be made to the other products. The summary table would show how each product performed in certain tasks. But once again, stress that this is not an official test, and that it only shows your experience with the product. Mention it shouldn't be taken as gospel.

Something you should consider doing to make the preview even more worthwhile is to ask your suppliers to help cover the cost of printing or postage. This is known as cooperative advertising or supplier subsidy.

The way it works is simple. The majority of suppliers calculate an advertising fee into the prices they charge you for their goods. This is designed to cover the cost of any advertising you run that promotes their products. Now your suppliers are unlikely to tell you this is the case. Obviously, if you don't ask for the money, they get to keep it. But they are usually happy to help with the cost of the advertising provided it's within reason.

Some suppliers won't give you money towards it, preferring to give you stock at cost. But let's face it; selling stock at a higher markup makes you more money anyway.

It's also worth mentioning they won't help you week in and week out. If you want them to help with a number of issues, put together a proposal with just one figure, rather than going back to them month after month.

Tips and Hints

I mentioned earlier that a product preview section is the second most exciting and well-read section you can put into any newsletter. The most exciting is easily a Tips and Hints section.

A lot of people worry whether or not their customers are going to read their newsletter, let alone act on it. The best way to ensure that they not only read it, but also look forward to each new issue (and even collect them), is to include some handy hints.

Imagine a hardware store that included a special section on how to prepare your house for painting, or how to lay pavers in your garden. This sort of free information is sure to be a winner, even with people who aren't looking to paint their house or put a path in their garden. Clients will hold onto this information so they can refer back to it at a later date.

A section like this has the added benefit of allowing you to showcase your expertise. By answering some of the many questions your clients have, you can show that for first-class information and advice, yours is the only store to turn to.

There is another more subtle benefit to be gained by including this section. It comes in the form of getting people to buy more products and embark on projects they might otherwise not have considered.

To give you an idea of how this might work, let's consider the hardware store again. Now if they were to include a spring article talking about painting the exterior of your home, and explaining that this is the best time to do it, there's a good chance people might "take the bait" and decide to do it. The article can then go on to list the best products to use, and include a special offer on some or all of them. Of course, when the unsuspecting customer comes into the store, the salesperson will be armed with a checklist of accessories that people will also need such as brushes, drop sheets, rollers, etc.

If you want your newsletter to be a success, try including a hints and tips section. It's bound to get your business flying.

Upcoming Events

People like to know what's going on, and they hate to miss out on something special. Therefore you should include an upcoming events section to let people know what's going on. There are a number of things you can include here, from upcoming sales and promotions to new products that are due for release soon.

If you don't have a lot of promotions throughout the year and struggle to find something to include, then maybe that's telling you something. You should really have no trouble finding two or three things to put in this section, but if you are having trouble, it's time to put your thinking cap on.

Promotions to mark certain seasons or to celebrate various sporting events give you the chance to draw people into your store and to make extra sales. That's what it's all about.

Introduce Your Team

One of the real benefits of newsletters is that they make your customers feel a part of what's happening in your business. They're not only being kept up-to-date with upcoming events and any changes to your stock or services, but they're thought enough of to receive your newsletter once every two or three months.

A good way to add to this feeling of being "part of the team" is by featuring your team members in a profile section. You see, people buy from people, not from companies. By letting them know a bit more about who they're dealing with, it makes them feel more comfortable buying from them. Your profile section does not have to be large; a couple of paragraphs are all that's required. But it can bring you some huge benefits. This is because not only does it make the customers feel like they know your team in a more personal way, but it also boosts your teams moral, and gives them a bit of a buzz. For this reason it's a good idea to include a photograph of your team member beside the article. You'll find out more about including photographs later.

You have the choice of a straight, biography-style column, or doing it a little more lightheartedly and running it as an interview. By this I mean you could ask your team member a series of questions, and then list the answers beside them. For example, what's his favorite food or movie? By putting a little thought into the questions, you can get some very amusing responses.

Another way to introduce your team is by having them write an article in your newsletter. This is a great way to demonstrate that your team really does know their stuff. Let's face it. If you write the whole thing yourself, people will think you're the expert and therefore, will only want to deal with you. By letting your team show off their skills, you'll improve their morale and lighten your workload.

Get Someone from Outside Your Company to Write a Section

In the past I've had many business owners complain to me that writing their newsletter takes up so much of their time. See, they all made the mistake of believing they had to write it all themselves. The main thing is not who writes it—just that it actually gets done.

As I've just mentioned, getting your team members to write a column takes some of the pressure off you, but there's another way that not only makes your life easier, but also gives your newsletter a bit of an edge.

Simply approach someone from an associated type of business and ask her to write the column for you. Now by associated business I don't mean one of your competitors. I mean someone who works in a similar field that can produce a relevant article.

To show you what I mean, imagine if you had a sporting goods store. You could approach a physical therapist, a sporting coach, and a fitness advisor to write expert articles for you. Just imagine how this would improve the readability of your newsletter. It would add an exciting new angle that would ensure that people read on.

Now you may be wondering why these people would bother writing something for your newsletter. But consider the benefits to them. They get to write to your entire database and demonstrate their expertise. If they're really smart, they'll approach you with an offer to get your customers into their business. For example, the physical therapist might offer a half-price treatment and checkup to anyone who buys a pair of sneakers from your store during the month of November.

So as you can see, the benefits to these people are unlimited. All you need to do is approach them with the offer and explain what it can do for them.

Humorous Section

It's all about getting people to read your articles and to take action. So understanding that this is the goal, you'll definitely get a better response if you include a "funnies" section.

Once again, this is a section that should not be too big. A quarter of a page is usually ample. In this section you have two choices for humorous stories.

The first choice is to have true stories. These can be things that have actually happened—that you've either heard of or had happen to you, or things that have happened to one of your customers.

The second choice is to have a few jokes. You can of course have both, but be careful you don't tell any jokes that might offend your clients. Also, try to keep them to stories and jokes that relate to your industry.

Customer Stories

Humorous stories are not the only input you can have from your customers. If yours is the type of business with a small, loyal customer base, then you might like to include a few stories that relate to them.

You can include things like congratulations on new births, engagements, or perhaps even promotions they've received at work. Listing some of their success stories may also make for good reading. Maybe they've just won a sporting event, or their child has just won a baby contest. Whatever it is, it's worth putting into your newsletter.

It's important that this section is kept small. While the person you're writing about will get a lift, you need to remember the idea is to make more sales. These types of stories usually don't put money in your bank.

One way you can make this section pay for itself is by including your customers' testimonials. Imagine if you owned a beauty clinic and you gave five lucky customers a facial product to try for six months. At the end of that time you could interview them to find out what they thought of the goods. By mentioning the success your customers have had with your product, you're sure to make more sales.

Sales Sections

You might have noticed we've spoken a lot about the sections that will get people reading your newsletter. But having them read it is pointless if in the end they don't buy. Understanding this, it's obvious your ads and selling messages are the most important parts of your newsletter.

You need to include a strong call to action in your ads (and even at the end of each article) that relates to a product or a service. If your articles have gotten them interested in buying, you need a call to action to actually get them in. A good way to accomplish this, and to actually work out if you're getting a good response from your newsletters, is to include a coupon.

Coupons are a great way to measure the success of your campaign. If you're not getting coupons back, then your newsletter is not working. Because many people will only skim through your articles, you need to have a strong offer in your coupon. People will normally read headlines first, the subheadlines next, and then finally the coupon.

You can often get people to go back and read the copy by making a strong, clear offer in your coupon. It may also be worthwhile to place an order form with your newsletter. But most importantly, you need to place a few ads in your newsletter. As I mentioned before, your newsletter is like your very own newspaper. Newspapers have ads, so why shouldn't your newsletter?

Let's have a look at the key points to writing your ads. You'll also find that many of these handy hints will apply to your articles and other sections as well.

Headline

The most important part of your advertisement is the headline. David Ogilvy, one of the all-time great direct-response copywriters, once said that 10 times as many people would read the headline as will read the rest of the ad. So if you get the headline wrong, you can kiss 90 percent of your advertising dollars good-bye.

One of the things you need to keep in mind is that the headline needs to take up at least 25 percent of your advertisement (or your article for that matter). Before you finalize your headlines, write down 10–20 options and ask your friends and team members which ones they like best. Then go with the most popular.

Typefaces

The typeface or font that you use in your newsletters and advertisements can make a big difference to the results you achieve. The two basic types are sans serif and serif fonts. Sans serif fonts don't have the little "feet" at the bottom of each letter. Serif fonts do. If you want people to read your articles, use a serif font.

Point Size

Studies have shown readership does not drop off between 14 and 7 point size. As a general rule, 10 points are ideal. Obviously the larger the font, the easier it is to read, so try to keep it as large as possible.

Highlighting Text

Use bold type to highlight key points in your body copy, headlines, and subheadlines.

Italics can also be used to highlight key areas of text, although it can be hard to read and should only be used sparingly. Never use all capitals. The only time you can is in a short headline, or for extra emphasis on single words.

To make your advertisement easier to read, break it up into paragraphs. Indenting your paragraphs, rather than leaving a line between them, can cut down on wasted space. Also consider using a drop cap first letter, as this is a great way to attract the eye of your reader.

Subheadlines

Subheadlines have three major benefits:

- They break up large blocks of text making them easier to read. If your article looks like one big "chunk" of text, it can put people off reading it. By using subheadlines you can break your copy up and give it some "space."

- They allow someone skimming over your newsletter to only read the points that interest them.
- They spark the reader's interest. If your headline doesn't get them in completely, you can get a second chance with your subheadlines.

It is important that your subheadlines tell a story. They need to convey your message to those just browsing through the newsletter.

Quotes and Pull Quotes

Just as subheadlines can get the reader to delve further into your copy, so too can a pull quote. This is a common technique used by magazines. What you do is to take an interesting passage, or a controversial statement, and place it in large type somewhere on the page.

Quite often the quote will have a line above and below it to help it stand out. It's also common for it to be placed in the middle of two columns of text, with a white space running around it to draw the eye in.

Here's an example of how it works:

They'll take an interesting passage, or a controversial statement, and place it in large type somewhere on the page.

As you can see, this certainly stands out and can tempt you to read on.

Another idea you might like to use in your newsletter is quotes from famous people. Once again, if you use a larger point (font) size, you can increase the chances of it being read. You should place these at the top or bottom of a page rather than in the middle, and always credit the author.

"Being good in business is the most fascinating kind of art."

—Andy Warhol

Body Copy

You only get one chance with a potential customer, so your first 50 words are crucial. You must arouse your readers' curiosity immediately with the very first paragraph. If they're not excited after the first 50 words, they won't read the rest of your article or ad.

Use the bare minimum of copy to get your message across; don't rattle on. But make sure you include enough information to get your reader interested enough to call you. If you're writing an ad, you should never tell the whole story. Tell them as much as you need to get them to call. By holding back some information you make it necessary for them to call to find out more.

As far as your ads go, they should tell a story and be easy to read. When you finish writing your ad, get someone to look over it and critique it for you. Only make one offer in your ad, and make it an exciting one.

Pictures

Studies have shown that ads containing a picture that takes up between 25 percent and 75 percent of the total advertisement have greater readership levels than those without one. You'll probably need to put a fair amount of text into your ad, so 25 percent is probably the ideal size.

Pictures are also an important part of any newsletter. People are generally very visual, and are therefore attracted to photographs. Note I said photographs, and not line drawings or clip art. You see, line art and clip art look tacky. People are used to seeing photographs, and they're far more attracted to them.

So wherever possible, you should always use photographs in your newsletter. The only exceptions should be small, humorous clip art pictures or line art in the form of technical drawings. For example, if you want to show the inner working of a new watch, you might use a cross-sectional line drawing to demonstrate the point you're trying to make.

Using real photographs can present a problem for some people. For starters, you'll need some way to place them electronically into your newsletter. Scanners are one way of doing this. A reasonable flatbed scanner will cost you less than $200. But if you didn't want to go to this expense (you still need to take the photo and have it developed in the first place), you could always ask a friend to scan it and save it onto a disk for you. Alternately there are companies who will scan pictures for you at a price. Many photo labs offer this service, but the feasibility of having this done will depend on how many pictures you're scanning a year, and how much each scan costs you. It may work out cheaper just to buy a scanner and be done with it.

Another way you can place photographs in your newsletter is by using a digital camera. Now a digital camera will cost you around $500, but you can rent them for much less. The trick here is to rent one for a day and take any pictures that you think you'll use over the course of the year. Now it obviously won't be possible to take photographs of all the new products you'll be previewing, as many of them won't have been released when you rent the camera. But for those few exceptions, it's probably worth getting them scanned by your local photo lab.

Always put a caption under your photo. Everybody reads the captions, so make sure you take advantage of this opportunity to get them to read your article.

While people will find your newsletter far more interesting if you include a few photographs, just throwing a few pictures in there won't work. You need to put some thought into the type of pictures and their positions.

Photographs of your premises (crowded restaurants or clubs) or your products are suitable for use in newsletters. The pictures need to back up your story. For example, a photograph of people having a great time in your club would help convince people that your establishment is a fun place to be.

You can also use photographs of people using your product or service. These can be used to educate them on what it is that you do. This can also be a great way to teach people how easy it is to use your product.

Consider putting a photograph of yourself in your newsletter. Again, people buy from people, not companies, so let them see the person behind the company name. Place your photograph so it looks straight out off the page or towards your body copy. If your picture is looking into the article, your potential customers will also be drawn into it.

Finding Out What Works

Before you put your ads into the newsletter, it's a good idea to test and measure them first. Test your headline and offer by running small ads in the classified section of your local paper and measuring the response. Test the response you get to each headline and each offer and then combine the best ones and run the ad in your newsletter.

Color

It could be argued that because people see in color, your newsletter should be printed in color. While this would seem a worthwhile argument, it pays to remember that most newspapers are printed in black and white.

Printing your newsletters in color will cost quite a bit more than standard black text on white paper. The aim of your newsletter is to bring customers in to your business, so the less you spend on attracting them, the better.

If your articles promise a benefit, your copy conveys your message, and your offer is worthwhile, it could be argued that you have no need for color. But most importantly, you need to ask yourself this: "Is my newsletter going to stand out well enough to be read, or will it go straight in to the trash?" This is something you'll have to guess to an extent, but it would pay, at least in the early stages, to keep the costs as low as possible.

If you were to use any color at all, you'd be well advised to print in full process color. Research has shown that the difference between two-color and black-and-white advertising material is minimal and doesn't justify the extra expenditure.

Printing on colored paper is an inexpensive way to brighten up your newsletter. But be careful which color paper you choose, as it can make your newsletter difficult to read.

Keep this in mind if you decide to print your text in color. As a general rule, you're far better off printing your text in black, as this will increase readability.

Layouts

You'll find a number of effective layouts in the examples that follow. When doing your layout, ask yourself this: How easy it is to read, and how easy is it to understand?

Many people fall into the trap of trying to jazz their newsletters up by adding different shapes and elements. Unless you have a good deal of artistic ability, you're best off sticking with a simpler layout. Putting your headline at the top, your coupon in the bottom right corner, and your pictures in the middle may not sound exciting, but it will generally bring better results.

Try to do your layout in blocks. By this I mean placing the headline, copy, pictures, and coupon in a blocked or balanced layout on the page. Keep your layout tight and don't leave too much empty space on the page. You're paying for these newsletters, so use every bit of them.

If you want your newsletter to look professional, you should pay a graphic designer to do it for you. Professional designers can be quite expensive. If you want to save some money, contact a college or university that runs a graphic design course. This way you may be able to find a second- or third-year student who will do it for a reasonable price.

You might also consider getting a graphic artist to do just the first layout for you. Once you have this, you can then use it as a template for any future newsletters.

Stock

Stock is the term used for the type of paper or card that you print your newsletters on. There are numerous types for you to choose from. Should you use glossy paper or plain paper? What about plain card or a textured card? These are just some of the questions to be answered when choosing your stock.

Just as there are a variety of materials, there are also a variety of prices, going from the very expensive to the downright cheap. But before deciding on the type of stock to use, you need to consider the type of product you're about to promote. If you're selling expensive, good-quality products, you'll need to use better-quality stock than you would for a cheaper product. You need to understand that by using high-quality stock, your prospects will believe yours is a high-quality product.

Printing

Another consideration in the creation of your newsletter is how to have it printed. This will depend largely on your budget and the type of product you're trying to sell. You basically have three choices:

- Professional printer: This is more expensive but ensures your newsletters will look first rate. Always have your newsletters professionally printed if your budget allows. This is a must for those higher-priced products.
- Personal printer: If you own, or have access to, a good-quality computer printer, you may be able to save on your printing cost. However, you need to keep in mind the quality of the stock you use, and the price of your product. If you were printing a large number of newsletters, it would probably be more cost effective in the long run to have them done professionally.
- Photocopies: This is the bargain basement of printing. If you decide to go with this option, make sure that the quality of reproduction is high. Having black lines all over your newsletters will make you, and your product, look cheap and nasty. Only use this option as a last resort.

Step 5: How Big Should Your Newsletter Be?

How much do you want to pay, and how much do you want to say? These are the two questions that will dictate how many pages your newsletter will consist of. The most common sizes for newsletters are between one and two pages, printed on both sides.

The decision can appear as simple as writing the articles, choosing the photos, and then working out the size of the ads and coupons. But there's a lot more to working out a size than most people think.

Usually, it's a case of how much you can afford for the printing.

But the question really should be how much you want to make. If the newsletter is good enough, it should make you money—not drain your funds. If you don't have a newsletter that you know works, you need to guess. You need to think about how many responses you need to "break even." That means, how many sales do you need to pay back the advertising cost?

Here's How You Work it Out

First, you need to work out your average profit. To do this, measure the amount of profit in each sale, every day for three days. Then find the average. If you want to skip the hard work, estimate this figure.

Next, get a few quotes on the cost of printing. Remember that the idea is to keep the costs as low as possible, so get as many quotes as you can. This of course won't be such an issue if you decide to photocopy your newsletters or run them off on your own printer.

Now divide the production cost by your average profit. This will give you the number of sales you need to pay for the newsletters.

Here's an Example

Let's say a hairdresser makes about $15 profit from each haircut. He spends around $270 getting his newsletter printed. That means he needs 18 new customers from his newsletters. Anything less and the newsletters are losing the business money.

Of course, it's not a hard-and-fast rule that you must break even on every newsletter. In the case of the hairdresser, he'd probably be happy with nine new loyal customers. After each customer has been in twice, he then becomes profitable.

This is called lifetime value—it's the amount a customer spends with you over the course of his lifetime. In the case of a business with a high level of repeat business (hairdresser, restaurant, mechanic, etc.), it might be worth losing money the first time, just to gain a new customer. This customer may ultimately be worth thousands.

If you get out of "break-even" thinking and into "lifetime value" mode, a whole new world of possibilities opens up. If you're confident you'll get these new customers back again, you can afford to offer something incredible and take a loss the first time they come in. Once you've established whether you have to break even, or if you can afford to rely on the lifetime value of the customer, you are then in a position to make a decision about size.

Step 6: How Often Should You Run Your Newsletter?

Quite simply, you should run a newsletter no less than once every three months. You see, what many people don't realize is that if you're not keeping in regular contact with your clients, they're no longer your clients. Another company will soon come in and make them feel special.

By keeping in contact with them on a regular basis, you'll ensure that they remain loyal to you and always keep you in the forefront of their minds.

If your only concern is the amount of time it takes to put your newsletter together, you should get your team to share the workload. It might even be an idea to get them to be editors on a rotational basis, where once a year a different team member puts it all together.

They would have to chase up the stories and the pictures and put them all together. You would then simply have to put together the ads, look over what they've done, and then get it printed. This would be an effective way to take the burden off you and still have it published on a regular basis.

Step 7: What Else Do You Need to Think About?

Use this section as a final checklist. Once you're happy with your newsletter, run through and make sure you're ready to get started. Here are a few things you may not have thought of.

Production: Make sure you check everything before it goes to print. Ask the printer for a "proof" (finished copy) and check it thoroughly. Don't let anything go out with spelling mistakes or (and yes, it does happen) the wrong phone number.

Phone Scripts: There are hundreds of cases where a newsletter made the phone ring off the hook, but the business owner saw very few sales at the end of the day. It all has to do with "conversion"—that is, how many enquiries you turn into sales. You need a script—a version of what you say to encourage people to buy when they phone or drop in. Just think about the best sales lines you've ever used, and compile them into one typed-up script.

Make sure you ask lots of "open-ended questions"—that is, questions that start with who, what, where, why, etc. Give a copy to every member of your team and make sure they *use* it. And of course, make sure your team knows that a newsletter has been sent out and to *expect* calls.

Check Stock and Team Levels: It's unlikely your newsletter will bring in hundreds of people (very few actually do), but you need to be prepared for a sizable response. There would be nothing worse than running a successful newsletter and then running out of stock, or being too busy to service these new enquiries.

Plan for the newsletter—and make sure you can cater for any increased demand.

Another thing I need to discuss are the things *not* to do when it comes to writing a newsletter. There are basically four key things you should never do.

Don't use your newsletter to:

- Push your own moral views and beliefs. Your customers are not interested in your opinions of how the world is a far worse place than it was 10 years ago. Nor do they have any desire to read your thoughts on the young of today and the evils of television. While it may seem tempting to "air your views" on certain subjects, to do so would be a recipe for disaster. Although some of your customers may share your views, there are others that will be offended by them. Understand that if you offend customers with something you write, they won't come back. However, if you don't write something that someone does agree with, they'll still keep coming to you.

- Put down your opposition. It's never good business to put down your opposition. It's far more likely to turn your customers against you, instead of against your competition. If you run a good, honest business, you have no need to take a shot at someone else. To do so will make people think that you've got something to hide. Remember, a lot of people like to see the underdog succeed. Don't give your opposition the advantage of being viewed in that light.

- Talk about yourself. Your newsletter is meant to be informative, and give your customers information of interest or benefit. Rambling on for page after page about your past experiences or achievements makes for very dull reading. In many cases it will turn your customers against you. Just stick to the things that interest your readers, not what interests you.

- Carry out personal vendettas. If someone has done the wrong thing by you, it can be tempting to put them down. But once again you need to understand this is simply not a good idea in the business world. Your customers just want to make a purchase from you and then get on with their lives. If they feel the next time they come into your store, they're going to be ear bashed about what a mongrel such and such is, they simply won't come in. It's best to stick to business and not enter into a public debate. Nobody wants to know about your personal problems.

Writing "Killer" Headlines

Writing a headline for an article is very similar to writing one for an advertisement. Both need to grab the reader's attention and then sell. Only one sells a product or service; the other sells an idea.

The headline of any article must sell the reader on the idea that it's worth taking the time to stop and read through it. One of the easiest ways for you to get a feel for writing effective headlines is to buy a number of newspapers and copy their style.

Writing headlines for different types of stories and businesses requires different styles. If you're writing for a retail store, your headline will be different than that if you're writing for a manufacturing firm. You also need to keep in mind where your story is to run, and whether or not you want your story to be factual or antagonistic.

Headline Starters

This is where you get to practice writing potential headlines for your articles. You'll get a sharper focus of what you want to really say to your readers, as well as learning what makes a headline work.

Quotes

First, write two headlines that make use of what someone else has said about your product or service. Here are some examples:

Leading authority claims George's Widgets are the best.

George's Widgets are market leaders, says expert.

Now it's your turn.

Leading Authority____

____

Expert Claims ____

____

Facts

Now try two headlines using research figures or facts to back up your story. Here are some examples:

Research shows that George's Widgets last longer.

Studies prove George's Widgets are best in market.

Now it's your turn.

Research shows ____

____

Studies prove ____

____

Here's how

Next, try two headlines beginning with "Here's how." Here are some good examples:

Here's how George's Widgets helps you live forever.

Here's how to get the perfect Widget—guaranteed.

Now it's your turn.

Here's how ____

____

Here's how ____

____

Company Name

Next, try two headlines beginning with your company's name. Here are some examples:

George's Widget store to extend trading hours.

George's Widget store to employ 35 locals.

Now it's your turn.

(Your company name) ______________________________________

____

(Your company name) ______________________________________

____

Announcement

Now try two headlines beginning with "Announcement." Here are some great examples:

Announcement to be made on extended trading hours for local retailers.

Announcement today on Widget exporters future.

Now it's your turn.

Announcement ____

____

Announcement ____

____

New

Now try two headlines beginning with "New." Here are some examples:

New widgets actually repair themselves.

New widget set to dominate market.

Now it's your turn.

New ______________________________

____

New ______________________________

____

Local

Last, try two headlines beginning with "Local." Here are some examples:

Local manufacturer to export widgets.

Local Widget manufacturer wins top award.

Now it's your turn.

Local ______________________________

____

Local ______________________________

____

As I've already mentioned, writing headlines for your articles is very similar to writing headlines for your ads. But there are some subtle differences. The best advertising headlines do three things: they identify the right target market, they provide benefits, and they generate enough interest to get people reading.

Let's look at each one of these in more depth.

Identify the Right Target Market: You need to make sure your target market sees and reads your ads. Your headline needs to immediately speak to them. There's nothing wrong with starting your headline with "MOTHERS" or even "ATTENTION Ladies 37-40 with no children." Of course, there are other more subtle ways, such as

"Here's how to make your Ford go faster" or "Help the kids succeed at school this year."

Provide Benefits: You need to give your readers reasons to investigate further. Think about it. What is really going to make them want to read on? A headline such as "MEN: How you can have twice as much sex as you're having now—guaranteed" speaks for itself. What can you say about your product or service? What is the main benefit? Once you've thought of that, try coming up with some more specific and interesting ways of phrasing it. For example, "How you can make an extra $4500 this year and pay off those credit card debts" is more interesting than "How you can make more money."

Generate Interest: There's nothing more powerful than curiosity. Compare these two headlines: "AMWAY: a new future for you" and "How you can make $1100 extra per week by meeting 3 new people per month." Both are for the same company, but one holds more interest value and is more likely to get you reading. Try getting the main benefit across without telling the whole story—and getting a bit of mystery in there too. Of course, too much mystery can kill your whole ad or article. Who'd read something with a headline such as "Pure grunt," "Big cheese" or "Stilted"? No one, as so many advertisers have discovered.

You've already written some test headlines for your articles, so now let's have a go at some for your ads. Try these:

7 reasons

First, write two headlines beginning with "7 reasons." Here are some examples:

7 reasons YOU should call George's Widgets today.

7 reasons to get your Widget from George's.

Now it's your turn.

7 reasons ____

____

7 reasons ____

____

Here's why

Now, try two headlines beginning with "Here's why." Here are some examples:

Here's why George's is offering YOU a FREE box of Widgets.

Here's why YOU need to call George's Widgets now.

Now it's your turn.

Here's why ____

____

Here's why ____

____

Here's how

Next, try two headlines beginning with "Here's how." Here are some good examples:

Here's how George's Widgets helps you live forever.

Here's how to get the perfect Widget—guaranteed.

Now it's your turn.

Here's how ____

____

Here's how ____

____

Announcing

Next, try two headlines beginning with "Announcing." Here are some examples:

Announcing . . . a Widget dealer that guarantees your delight.

Announcing . . . a guaranteed way to lose weight using Widgets.

Now it's your turn.

Announcing ____

____

Announcing ____

____

DON'T

Now try two headlines beginning with "DON'T." Here are some great examples:

DON'T take another breath until you read this.

DON'T call anyone about Widgets until YOU speak to George's.

Now it's your turn.

DON'T ____

____

DON'T ____

____

Now

Last, try two headlines beginning with "Now." Here are some examples:

Now available . . . home hairdressing kits that your teenage daughter will like.

Now in preproduction . . . a movie based on the life of Elvis Presley.

Now it's your turn.

Now ____

____

Now ____

____

Offers

What Works and What Doesn't?

So you've written a great headline, an exciting first paragraph, and subheadlines that tell a story. But what are you going to do to get your target market to respond? Great articles alone will not work; you need to have a strong offer, an offer you would respond to.

So What Is a Great Offer?

When thinking of what to offer your customers, ask yourself this: "If I read this ad or article, would the offer be good enough to make me respond?" If the answer is no, then go back to the drawing board. Without a great offer, you cannot achieve great results.

Another thing to consider when coming up with your offer is the lifetime value of the people who respond to your ad. Taking a smaller profit in the short term will generally work out better in the long run.

Here are some examples of powerful offers:

- Free haircut—For a hairdressing salon looking to increase its database.
- 2 Steak Dinners and 2 Glasses of Wine for $10—Restaurant recruiting members for its VIP Club.
- 1 New Release Video and a Large Pizza for $6—Video store promotion to recruit new members.

All of these offers are worthwhile and sure to get a great response. Weak offers will cause your ad to fail. Understand that your offer is the part of your ad and gets your customers to act now and to buy from you rather than your opposition.

Here are some examples of weak offers:

- 10% Off—This is not a big enough discount to generate interest.
- Call now for your free color brochure—So what?
- Buy 9 and get the 10th for 1/2 price—No one would respond to this offer.

Types of Offers

Here are some offers that would be worth considering:

The Added Value with Soft Dollar Cost

Soft dollar cost refers to products, services or added extras that you can combine with your standard product to make it more attractive and increase its perceived value, without adding much, if anything, to your costs.

For this strategy to be effective, the added extra must have a high perceived value. In other words, your customers must see the added benefit as being great value.

The Package Offer

By packaging products and services together, you create a more marketable combination. There is a higher perceived value when products or services are packaged. Your customers will want to buy more, simply because of the extra products they get when buying a product they already want. One of the best examples of a great package is computer equipment. Buy the hardware and receive the software for free. This style of offer is very attractive to potential customers.

Discounts versus Bonus Offers

More often than not, discounting will cost you profits. A far better way of clearing stock and generating extra trade is to have a "2 for the price of 1" sale. Or, try a "buy one of these and get one of these FREE" type of sale. The other way of putting this is every 10th purchase free, or when you spend $100, we'll give you $20 off your next purchase.

Valued at Offer

If you are including a free item in your ad, make sure you put a value on it. For example, CALL now for your FREE consultation, normally valued at $75. This positions your time, product, or service much more than a simple free giveaway people won't value or appreciate would.

Time-Limited Offers

Place a time limit on your offer. It will dramatically increase the response rate you get because it gives people a reason to respond right now. Place urgency in your offer. Say, "For a short time only" . . . "Call before Tuesday" . . . "Only while stocks last." These will all create a sense of urgency in your consumer's mind.

Guarantee Offers

Using a guarantee offer is a great way to boost the response to your ad. People will be far more willing to part with their money if you take the risk out of the buying decision. The better the guarantee you make, the higher your response will be.

Free Offers

Giving away something absolutely free, with no catches whatsoever, is often a brilliant way to build a loyal customer base. Offer a "bribe" to get them in the door initially, then great service and products to encourage them to come back. This type of offer can reduce your cost per lead dramatically.

"So there it is in a nutshell, Charlie. Do you still feel you shouldn't consider a newsletter of your own?"

"I must say, Brad, you've put a whole new spin on them. I think I could produce my own, and I might seriously think about it. Obviously it's not something I can decide on here and now, is it?"

"No, and I wouldn't expect you to. Think about it over the next few days, and if you decide to, you'll know exactly how to go about it. Refer back to the notes you made this morning, and you'll be right."

"Want some coffee?" he asked, flicking the switch of the kettle on. I nodded, and continued.

"Charlie, I'm going to leave you a few templates so that if you decide to produce your own newsletter, it'll be even easier. Why reinvent the wheel?"

"Fantastic. Would you like a muffin as well?"

Examples

This time I'm going to give you some templates to get you going. Just fill in the text and pictures. There are also many software packages available; you might even have some already loaded as templates into your computer.

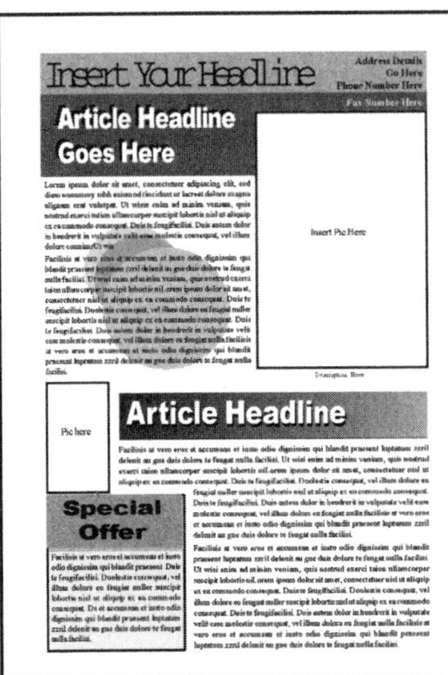

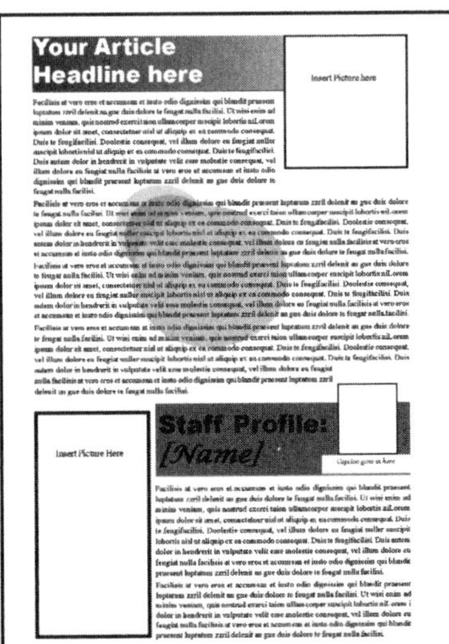

Your Headline

Issue 0, Month 0000

Greg Norris

'Why YOU need to' style of headline goes here ...

Facilisis at vero eros et accumsan et iusto odio dignissim qui blandit praesent luptatum zzril delenit au gue duis dolore te feugat nulla facilisi. Ut wisi enim ad minim veniam, quis nostrud exerci taion ullamcorper suscipit lobortis niLorem ipsum dolor sit amet, consectetuer nisl ut aliquip ex ea commodo consequat. Duis te feugifacilisi. Doolestie consequat, vel illum dolore eu feugiat nuller suscipit lobortis nisl ut aliquip ex ea commodo consequat. Duis te feugifacilisi. Duis autem dolor in hendrerit in vulputate velit esse molestie consequat, vel illum dolore eu feugiat nulla facilisis at vero eros et accumsan et iusto odio dignissim qui blandit praesent luptatum zzril delenit au gue duis dolore te feugat nulla facilisi.

Facilisis at vero eros et accumsan et iusto odio dignissim qui blandit praesent luptatum zzril delenit au gue duis dolore te sit amet, consectetuer nisl ut aliquip ex ea commodo consequat. Duis te feugifacilisi. Doolestie consequat, vel illum dolore eu feugiat nuller suscipit lobortis nisl ut aliquip ex ea commodo consequat. Duis te feugifacilisi. Duis autem dolor in hendrerit in vulputate velit esse molestie consequat, vel illum dolore eu feugiat nulla facilisis at vero eros et accumsan et iusto odio dignissim qui blandit praesent luptatum zzril delenit au gue duis dolore te feugat nulla facilisi.

Article Headline Here ...

Facilisis at vero eros et accumsan et iusto odio dignissim qui blandit praesent luptatum zzril delenit au gue duis dolore te feugat nulla facilisi. Ut wisi enim ad minim veniam, quis nostrud exerci taion ullamcorper suscipit lobortis niLorem ipsum dolor sit amet, consectetuer nisl ut aliquip ex ea commodo consequat. Duis te feugifacilisi. Doolestie consequat, vel illum dolore eu feugiat nuller suscipit lobortis nisl ut aliquip ex ea commodo consequat. Duis te feugifacilisi. Duis autem dolor in hendrerit in vulputate velit esse molestie consequat, vel illum dolore eu feugiat nulla facilisis at vero eros et accumsan et iusto odio dignissim qui blandit praesent luptatum zzril delenit au gue duis dolore te feugat nulla facilisi.

Facilisis at vero eros et accumsan et iusto odio dignissim qui blandit praesent luptatum zzril delenit au gue duis dolore te feugat nulla facilisi. Ut wisi enim ad minim veniam, quis nostrud exerci taion ullamcorper suscipit lobortis niLorem ipsum dolor sit amet, consectetuer nisl ut aliquip ex ea commodo consequat. Duis te feugifacilisi. Doolestie consequat, vel illum dolore eu feugiat nuller suscipit lobortis nisl ut aliquip ex ea commodo consequat. Duis te feugifacilisi. Duis autem dolor in hendrerit in vulputate velit esse molestie consequat, vel illum dolore eu feugiat nulla facilisis at vero eros et accumsan et iusto odio dignissim qui blandit praesent luptatum zzril delenit au gue duis dolore te feugat nulla facilisi.

ARTICLE HEADLINE

Facilisis at vero eros et accumsan et iusto odio dignissim qui blandit praesent luptatum zzril delenit au gue duis dolore te feugat nulla facilisi. Ut wisi enim ad minim veniam, quis nostrud exerci taion ullamcorper suscipit lobortis niLorem ipsum dolor sit amet, consectetuer nisl ut aliquip ex ea commodo consequat. Duis te feugifacilisi. Doolestie consequat, vel illum dolore eu feugiat nuller suscipit lobortis nisl ut aliquip ex ea commodo consequat. Duis te feugifacilisi. Duis autem dolor in hendrerit in vulputate velit esse molestie consequat, vel illum dolore eu feugiat nulla facilisis at vero eros et accumsan et iusto odio dignissim qui blandit praesent luptatum zzril delenit au gue duis dolore te feugat nulla facilisi.

Facilisis at vero eros et accumsan et iusto odio dignissim qui blandit praesent luptatum zzril delenit au gue duis dolore te feugat nulla facilisi. Ut wisi enim ad minim veniam, quis nostrud exerci taion ullamcorper suscipit lobortis niLorem ipsum dolor sit amet, consectetuer nisl ut aliquip ex ea commodo consequat. Duis te feugifacilisi. Doolestie consequat, vel illum dolore eu feugiat nuller suscipit lobortis nisl ut aliquip ex ea commodo consequat.

Facilisis at vero eros et accumsan et iusto odio dignissim qui blandit praesent luptatum zzril delenit au gum, quis nostrud exerci taion ullamco. Doolestie consequat, vel illum dolore eu feugiat nuller suscipit lobortis nisl ut aliquip ex ea commodo consequat. Duis te feugifacilisi. Duis autem dolor in hendrerit in vulputate velit esse molestie consequat, vel illum dolore eu feugiat nulla facilisis at vero eros et accumsan et iusto odio dignissim qui blandit praesent luptatum zzril delenit au gue duis dolore te feugat nulla facilisi.

Article Headline Goes Here

Facilisis at vero eros et accumsan et iusto odio dignissim qui blandit praesent luptatum zzril delenit au gue duis dolore te feugat nulla facilisi. Ut wisi enim ad minim veniam, quis nostrud exerci taion ullamcorper suscipit lobortis niLorem ipsum dolor sit amet, consectetuer nisl ut aliquip ex ea commodo consequat. Duis te feugifacilisi. Doolestie consequat, vel illum dolore eu feugiat nuller suscipit lobortis nisl ut aliquip ex ea commodo consequat. Duis te feugifacilisi. Duis autem dolor in hendrerit in vulputate velit esse molestie consequat, vel illum dolore eu feugiat nulla facilisis at vero eros et accumsan et iusto odio dignissim qui blandit praesent luptatum zzril delenit au gue duis dolore te feugat nulla facilisi.

Facilisis at vero eros et accumsan et iusto odio dignissim qui blandit praesent luptatum zzril delenit au gue duis dolore te feugat nulla facilisi. Ut wisi enim ad minim veniam, quis nostrud exerci taion ullamcorper suscipit lobortis niLorem ipsum dolor sit amet, consectetuer nisl ut aliquip ex ea commodo consequat. Duis te feugifacilisi. Doolestie consequat, vel illum dolore eu feugiat nuller suscipit lobortis nisl ut aliquip ex ea commodo consequat. Duis te feugifacilisi. Duis autem dolor in hendrerit in vulputate velit esse molestie consequat, vel illum dolore eu feugiat nulla facilisis at vero eros et accumsan et iusto odio dignissim qui blandit praesent luptatum zzril delenit au gue duis dolore te feugat nulla facilisi.

Your Guarantee, or special offer goes here. make sure you include your contact details, and ensure that the offer is powerful enough to pull a response ...

Place Your Headline here

Facilisis at vero eros et accumsan et iusto odio dignissim qui blandit praesent luptatum zzril delenit au gue duis dolore te feugat nulla facilisi. Ut wisi enim ad minim veniam, quis nostrud exerci taion ullamcorper suscipit lobortis niLorem ipsum dolor sit amet, consectetuer nisl ut aliquip ex ea commodo consequat. Duis te feugifacilisi. Doolestie consequat, vel illum dolore eu feugiat nuller suscipit lobortis nisl ut aliquip ex ea commodo consequat. Duis te feugifacilisi. Duis autem dolor in hendrerit in vulputate velit esse molestie consequat, vel illum dolore eu feugiat nulla facilisis at vero eros et accumsan et iusto odio dignissim qui blandit praesent luptatum zzril delenit au gue duis dolore te feugat nulla facilisi.

Facilisis at vero eros et accumsan et iusto odio dignissim qui blandit praesent luptatum zzril delenit au gue duis dolore te feugat nulla facilisi. Ut wisi enim ad minim vequat. Duis te feugifacilisi. Duis autem dolor in hendrerit in vulputate velit esse molestie consequat, vel illum dolore eu feugiat nulla facilisis at vero eros et accumsan et iusto odio dignissim qui blandit praesent luptatum zzril delenit au gue duis dolore te feugat nulla facilisi.

Facilisis at vero eros et accumsan et iusto odio dignissim qui blandit praesent luptatum zzril delenit au gue duis dolore te feugat nulla facilisi. Ut wisi enim ad minim veum dolore eu feugiat nuller suscipit lobortis nisl ut aliquip ex ea commodo com dolor in hendrerit in vulputate velit esse molestie consequat, vel illum dolore eu feugiat nulla facilisis at vero eros et accumsan et iusto odio dignissim qui blandit praesent luptatum zzril delenit au gue duis dolore te feugat nulla facilisi.

Place Special Offer headline Here

Facilisis at vero eros et accumsan et iusto odio dignissim qui blandit praesent luptatum zzril delenit au gue duis dolore te feugat nulla facilisi. Ut wisi enim ad minim vensi. Doolestie consequat, vel illum dolore eu feugiat nuller suscipit lobortis nisl ut aliquip ex ea commodo consequat. Duis te feugifacilisi. Duis autem dolor in hendrerit in vulputate velit esse molestie consequat, vel illum dolore eu feugiat nulla facilisis at vero eros et accumsan et iusto odio dignissim qui blandit praesent zzril delenit au gue duis dolore te feugat nulla facilisi.

Part 2

Closed-Door Sales

This part of the book is your do-it-yourself guide to running special after-hours sales that generate cashflow—fast!

Once you've read through it, you should know exactly how to put together powerful invitation letters, how to plan the evening, and how make more sales than you thought possible. More importantly, you'll have a selection of marketing pieces to get you started.

The aim here is to give you a *complete* strategy, from start to finish. You'll learn everything you need to know in order to run a super successful closed-door sale.

This is the next step in your marketing success story. From this point on, you'll have the skills to make closed-door sales work for you. I personally guarantee it.

A Note about Testing and Measuring

The greatest businesspeople and marketers are not necessarily the smartest or most innovative. Most simply understand the concept of testing and measuring.

When you are testing and measuring, there is no "failure" (except the failure to record and analyze your results). Every step brings you one step closer to the right formula, and the right approach.

If you approach your marketing expecting everything to work first time, you'll be bitter and twisted when you discover it doesn't. You may give up before you should. *Remember this:* marketing has certain rules, but it's still largely trial and error. You give it your best guess, and then find out for sure.

It's essential that you meticulously record every result. It's extra work, but you'll be glad when you have a marketing strategy that you know will produce results. That confidence only comes from testing and measuring.

When it comes to closed-door sales, it can be difficult to test. There are two reasons for this.

First, you don't know how well your sale is going to go until you actually run it for real. There isn't really a way to run it on a small scale, see how many responses you get, and then do it bigger.

Secondly, if you run a closed-door sale, invite everyone, and it bombs, it's not always the best idea to run another one soon after. People may get the impression your "special" sale wasn't really that special. This can take the power out of the strategy and put a strain on your credibility.

So what's the answer?

You need to find other ways to test. For example, you can write your invitation letter, plan the sale, then share the concept with a few trusted customers. Ask whether they'd really come, and find out whether they'd tell other people about it.

A great question to ask is this: "So assuming you had something important on the night of the sale, what would I have to say in this letter to encourage you to cancel your plans and come?" That always generates an interesting response.

It's important to bear in mind that people are fickle, forgetful, and generally scatterbrained. They may fully intend to come to your sale, but forget or be distracted at the last minute. You have to find out what kind of appeal will really make an *impact* on your customers.

The best way to discover this is simply to ask them before going ahead with the closed-door sale.

The Nature of Closed-Door Sales

"OK, Charlie," I continued, eager to press on. I knew that this strategy would be new to him. I also knew he would immediately grasp its potential.

"What I'm now going to discuss is a powerful strategy that involves inviting your best customers around for a closed-door sale. By this I mean a sale that's not open to the public, just to invited customers. It not only makes them feel special, it also is a great way to move stock, especially slow-moving stock."

"Brad, this garage isn't a department store, you know," he quipped and burst out laughing. He liked to poke fun at me every now and then, but I didn't mind. The business environment is supposed to be fun.

"There's no reason why you couldn't adopt some of their strategies and techniques, you know. Doing so is sure to set you apart from your competition, and that's one of the things you should be aiming for. You see, you have an ideal setup here for a closed-door sale. Imagine a workshop full of car enthusiasts all talking cars, meeting other like-minded people and socializing over a glass of beer. Think of the business you could do in that atmosphere, Charlie! You could lay on a technical demonstration or presentation from a manufacturer or racing team. You could invite an oil company to talk about the benefits of synthetic oil, for instance, and then one lucky customer could win a lubrication hamper courtesy of the oil company. Think of the business you could rack up in one night! Not only could you sell product, you could also take bookings for services or performance tuning work. And think of the networking you and your customers could do. You could turn this into a regular event with different topics being discussed each time."

"Now you've got me excited, Brad. You're talking my language. I could do all that, and more. What about an evening for the ladies? Explaining to them the basics of car maintenance. Or what about a session on modifications? Or how about a day at the race track? I'm excited."

"I thought this would get you going. And, of course, you could tie this strategy in with your newsletter and you VIP Club. The potential is limitless. So, let's start, shall we?"

"Fire away, Brad. I'm listening."

What Is a Successful Closed-Door Sale?

Before getting started, it's important to understand what we're aiming for. Without knowing what success is, it's hard to achieve it.

Most business people tend to have unrealistic expectations. They think 90 percent of their customers will come to their closed-door sale, and that all will spend big dollars.

The reality is most closed-door sales only achieve a fraction of that result. On average, one in five people will attend a closed-door sale, and about half won't buy anything of any significance.

So Does That Make the Exercise a Failure?

Not necessarily. Basically, any closed-door sale that makes you money should be considered successful. That means, if you take in more money than you shell out, the closed-door sale has been worth the trouble.

Before planning your sale, there are a few things you need to do.

1. **Work out your costs.** This includes the cost of printing, envelopes, the price of any giveaways, team costs, and so on.

2. **Know your margins.** You need to know the net profit you make from each item. By understanding how much you actually make from each sale, you'll be able to work out the number of sales required to make your sale profitable.

After your sale is over, you will have a much better idea of whether it was successful or not. Add up the total amount of profit, and then balance that against the amount you had to spend to make the sale worthwhile.

Of course, sometimes the aim of a closed-door sale is purely to clear out old stock that's really just taking up space. In this case, it's no big deal if you don't make a profit—you'll be achieving something if you turn that old unwanted stock into cash.

Sometimes, old stock is better off being sold for half price. You've already paid for it, and it's tying up your funds. If you sell it quickly and bring in cashflow, you can divert your resources to a more profitable line.

What Makes a Successful Closed-Door Sale?

Now that we understand what a successful closed-door sale is, it's a good idea to take a broad overview and consider the key elements of a sale that really produces results.

Invitation Letter: Your invitation letter should create real excitement and make people want to cancel whatever plans they had to come to your sale.

Offers: If you're not offering people a real incentive to come, it's unlikely they will. Your offers (or specials) need to be truly enticing. It's common to have a number of 'loss leaders' to get people in the door—these are items you sell for well below cost.

Customer Service: If your team just stands around at the sale, looking disappointed because they're missing *Melrose Place* on television, people will be unlikely to really spend. You need to greet people warmly, help them find what they're looking for, then really make an effort to sell them something.

Social Occasion: The best closed-door sales are the ones that turn into a miniparty. People come with friends, stay around to eat your snacks, and walk out with an armful of purchases. Of course, not every business will have the opportunity to create this vibe, but it's something to aim for. Just think of it like this. You're inviting hundreds of friends over. How are you going to give them a good time and make sure they stay?

I'm now going to teach you much more about every aspect of closed-door sales. You're going to discover how to write invitation letters that stop people in their tracks, how to run amazing specials without going broke, and how to make the absolute most out of every customer who turns up at your sale. And that's really only the beginning.

You'll find out that running a successful closed-door sale is as easy as following a well-established formula. The system you'll learn has been used by hundreds of businesses with great success, and it's almost certain to work for you as well. Let's get started.

The Six Steps to Running a Profitable Closed-Door Sale

Step 1: Why Run a Closed-Door Sale?

It may seem strange to start with the question like this. Especially considering that you're reading this, you might be pretty convinced this strategy is for you.

Even so, it's a good idea to identify the precise reason you are running this sale. Once we know that, it's simple to work out how you can go about achieving your ultimate goal. As we discussed before, you can't succeed without first knowing what success is.

Let's take a look at the different reasons businesses run closed-door sales for their customers.

Quick Cashflow: Sometimes a closed-door sale is an excellent way to boost the month's sales, and quickly. I know of one business that runs regular closed-door sales, and tends to turn over more in one night than they do in an average month. If this is your aim, you're going to need to concentrate on profit margins. There's not really much point in selling stock below cost so you can partly pay your supplier bills. While the aim is to get cash in the door, you will only be harming your business if you sell things too cheaply. Remember, the only money you make is the *profit.*

A Treat for Your Customers: Some businesses run closed-door sales purely as a special bonus for their customers. It's like a reward for their loyalty. These type of closed-door sales always work. Whether people come to your sale or not, they'll feel special just because you invited them. You can really play on this in your invitation letter. All closed-door sales achieve these objectives to some degree, but if it's your stated main aim, you can really get the feeling across.

Referrals: This is truly one of the cleverest reasons to run a closed-door sale. You invite all your customers and make the price of entry to the sale one friend who has never bought from our business before. That's right. If people want to come along and check out the awesome specials and bargains, they have to bring friends along. Not only will the friends probably buy something, boosting your takings for the night, there's a good chance they'll become regular customers, especially if they enjoy themselves and liked the stock you offer. Often, you'll hear your customers' friends say, "I normally go to [one of your competitors], but they never have anything like this." That's precisely the kind of response you want to elicit. The friends start to believe they've been missing out.

Clear Old Stock: Sometimes, running a closed-door sale is a great way to get rid of all that stock you've had forever, yet can't seem to sell. There's something about a special sale that puts people in a buying mood. Even if you've advertised an item for below cost and had it on display with a big, red half-price sign, you still have a better chance of selling it at a closed-door sale. I remember one music store I worked with had this one particular guitar in stock for more than two years. It was an expensive and high-quality model, and it was really quite good value for the price. Anyway, the store had tried virtually everything to sell it, with no success. Ultimately, the team started believing it had some kind of weird curse on it. They'd actually tried to sell if for about 70 percent of the *cost* price, and still had no takers. Then they ran a closed-door sale. They went for a more moderate discount—25 percent off the retail price. Within the first 30 minutes of the sale, it was gone. Although they didn't really make any money from selling the guitar, they turned the instrument into cash, which could then be used to pay the bills and buy new stock.

Step 2: When Should You Run Your Sale?

Most business owners never really give this question enough thought, mistakenly thinking that if they set the time, people will find a way to get there.

Now while this may sometimes be true, it's more often correct to suggest people will come to your sale only if it's *convenient*. That means, if they can stop by on their way home from work, or drop in just after dinner, they'll come.

If they have to put other things aside and go to a lot of trouble to make it to your sale, your chances of success diminish.

To work out which day or night and what time, you first have to consider who your customers are. Do they work during the day? Do they have to prepare a meal for the family? Can they drive, or will somebody be driving them? Are they night owls, or do they go to bed early? Are they likely to be busy on any particular night?

Of course, it's going to vary from customer to customer, but you should be able to develop a profile that fits most people who regularly do business with you.

As a general guideline, it's best to have your sale on a weeknight. Most people don't make plans for their weeknights, preferring just to bum around and watch TV. Although they may be unhappy about missing their favorite show to come to your sale, they can always put a tape in the VCR and watch it when they come home.

Sales planned for Thursday, Friday, Saturday, or Sunday nights are usually not a good idea. People do particular things on these nights and are unlikely to want to change their plans.

Monday nights are not recommended either. For some reason, people almost always want to keep Monday night free, as if they need extra time and space to recover after the first day of the week.

That leaves Tuesday and Wednesday. The choice is yours, although I have a definite preference towards Wednesday. When it gets to Wednesday night, people tend to get happier—they feel the week is drawing to a close, and they feel a little more free.

By the way, I don't buy into all of this nonsense. If you live 5 days of the week waiting for the other 2, you're wasting 5/7 of your life. Having said that, it's undeniable that many people live this way, and probably will forever.

When deciding on a time for your sale, you have three choices—early and short, early and long, or late and short.

The safest option is early and long—that means your sale starts early (say around 5:30 p.m.) and goes for a long time (four or five hours).

Sometimes it's better to run the sale late so people have a chance to get home, eat dinner, get changed, and then come out. This will often work better because people feel relaxed. They don't have anywhere to go or anything to do. This is especially true when it comes to mothers.

The only time you should run an early and short sale is when you are dealing with people on their way home from work. For example, if your business is in the city's business district and the majority of your customers are city workers who live in the suburbs, you should definitely run an early sale. It's extremely unlikely they will go all the way home, then come all the way back again. Regardless of how good your specials are, people just can't be bothered going to that much effort.

Aside from the weeknight option, here are some other times you might like to consider.

Saturday Morning: If you're not normally open on Saturday morning, running your sale at this time can work incredibly well. People are probably out doing their shopping anyway, so stopping in at your sale is no drama. They'll plan it into their schedule. The same goes for Thursday night, although this tends to be less successful.

Sunday Morning: This can work well also, but you'll find your customers will be in a different frame of mind. People tend to completely lose all sense of focus on Sundays and they're generally not in the mood for running around looking for a great deal. Of course, there are plenty of exceptions to that rule.

Weekday Lunchtime: If your business is centrally located and most of your customers are workers who don't live in the area, a lunchtime sale can work well. However, many people don't have complete control over when they take their lunch break, meaning they may miss most of your sale. If you're going to do this, run the sale from 11:45 a.m. until 2:00 p.m.

Step 3: What Should You Offer?

If your sale is really going to succeed, you're going to need great specials and offers.

People may come because they feel special, but they won't buy unless you've got something that they perceive to be a real, once-in-a-lifetime bargain.

So how do you get these great bargains and still make money?

If you own a retail store, you'd already have plenty of ideas. You've probably run dozens of sales in your time as a business owner, and a closed-door sale is no different.

First stop is your suppliers. Ask them what they're willing to do for you in exchange for a little extra exposure. Not only will you be introducing plenty of new customers to their products through the sale, you'll also be helping your suppliers to increase their figures.

After that, do a stock take and work out all the things that have been hanging around too long. Sacrifice these items at cost or below, then resolve to never buy those lines again.

Then look at your everyday items and think about the kind of deals you could offer.

Remember that people aren't stupid. If you offer great deals on a line that is totally unpopular, yet none on the products people really want, your customers will quickly judge the sale to be a waste of time. They either won't come, or they'll leave quickly.

You don't have to simply reduce the price. There are more creative ways to come up with a great deal. Consider these:

The Added Value with Soft Dollar Cost

Soft dollar cost refers to products, services or added extras you can combine with your standard product to make it more attractive and increase its perceived value, without adding much, if anything, to your costs. For this strategy to be effective, the added extra must have a high perceived value. Your customers must see the added benefit as being great value.

The Package Offer

By packaging products and services together, you create a more marketable combination. There is a higher perceived value when products or services are packaged. Your customers will want to buy more, simply due to the extra products they get when buying a product they already want.

Discounts versus Bonus Offers

More often than not, discounting will cost you profits. A far better way of clearing stock and generating extra trade is to have a "2 for the price of 1" deal. Or, try a "buy one of these and get one of these FREE" offer.

FREE Offers

Giving away something absolutely free, with no catches whatsoever, is often a brilliant way to get people to your sale. Offer a "bribe" to get them in the door initially, then great service and other good deals to encourage them to buy more.

Spend Over $X

This is where you offer people something free if they spend more than a certain amount at your sale. For example, you could get a bunch of items from a supplier at a great price. Offer your customers the pick of these if they spend more than

$100. It's usually a good idea to use this as an additional offer, rather than your main hook.

Host Beneficiary

This is an excellent way to give added value without losing profits. You approach another business, for example a hairdresser. Say to the hairdresser, "I like the way you do business. I'd like to refer all my customers to you. If I could give them a voucher for a free haircut, I'm sure they'd definitely come, and I'm certain they'd become regular clients. You'd have to do a few free cuts, but you'd get heaps of new customers out from it." You then do this with two or three other businesses, and give out these vouchers as bonuses with any purchase.

It pays to remember that simply asking people to act now (or for that matter, telling them to act now) is rarely enough. You need to give them a good reason why *now* is the time to buy something.

See, most purchases can be delayed forever. It's one thing to create desire, but it's another to actually get people to part with their cash. Remember what I said previously about rearranging people's buying priorities?

Step 4: How Will You Write an Invitation Letter That Works?

It's a common misconception that you have to be a great writer, or some wizard with words, to write a letter that works. That's rubbish. People who know who they're writing to and how to come up with a good offer can write successful letters. Their writing skills are irrelevant.

Simply writing to your database and saying, "We're having a special sale, customers only. Everything will be half price," is enough. It doesn't matter what words you use, or even if you make spelling mistakes. It might sound funny, but most people won't even notice.

At the end of the day, people won't buy from you just because you can write good letters. By the same token, people probably won't avoid buying from you because you can't spell.

As long as your message is clear, quick, and well targeted, your letter will work. There is only one sin you don't want to commit, and that's getting off the point, or rambling on too long. If every word and every sentence says something important about the sale and why the prospect should buy, fine. If your letter is full of guff, people will lose interest very quickly. The same applies if you stray from your initial intention and message.

Here are some other guidelines for getting your letter just right:

Your headline: Tell people exactly what they will achieve by reading the letter. The headline lets prospects know whether they should bother reading on. It needs to promise immediate benefits. You should say something like, "You're invited to our special sale—you'll save up to 90 percent on everything in store, and have access to the very latest products." It's a good idea to include some details about the bargains being offered.

Create a strong introduction: The first couple of sentences are incredibly important. They tell people whether they should read on in depth or start skimming. Nine times out of 10 they'll skim (or trash the letter entirely). Of course, in most cases your first paragraph will just support your headline. For example, "You're probably a little disbelieving. In fact, I'm certain you think I'm pulling your leg, but let me assure you—that headline is 100% true."

Include a strong, specific call to action: If you don't tell people what to do, they probably won't do anything. Give them precise instructions on what to do—whom to call, which number to use, when to do it, and what to ask for. Here's a good example: "Call Gordon Harris now at 345-6756 and let us know you'll be at the sale." Then give very precise details on when the sale is, where and how to get there. Remember, some people on your database may not have bought from you for ages, so a map is appropriate.

Include concise and convincing body copy: The body copy is the actual text between the introduction and the call to action. You don't need to be a great writer to do this part well; it's more important you get the point across clearly, in as few words as possible, and in a logical order. After you write your first draft, go through and edit viciously. Cut out any sentence or word that doesn't need to be there. Next, read it aloud and make sure it flows. Have a couple of people check it through, and ask them to tell you what they got out of it. Ask them to explain it back to you, just to make sure you're getting your point across. Ask which parts were boring, and don't be afraid of criticism. You didn't set out to be the world's greatest writer anyway, so any comments should be helpful, not hurtful.

Use a P.S.: One of the most important aspects of the copy is the P.S. In fact, the P.S. is often the most read part of the letter. It pays to include a major point right at the end. For example, details of the special lucky door prize you'll be giving away at the sale.

Make the layout fun: When writing your letter, forget everything you learned at school about writing a so-called "business letter." Indent paragraphs, splash bold throughout, use bullet points, and give everything lots of space. And don't make your letter too long or too short, but remember, the number of pages is less important than the actual layout. So if spacing it out spills the letter over three pages instead of one, that's OK as long as it's fun to read. There's a common perception that a one- page letter will always be read. That's not strictly true. You see, if the letter is packed solid with text just so it'll fit on one page, people will be more turned off than if it was four spaced pages. Likewise, if it doesn't have enough meat (reasons to act), people won't do anything. You need to say enough to inspire them to do something, but not so much that they run out of time, or get bored.

Avoid anything that's hard to read: Type your letter in a standard font: Times New Roman or Courier. While some fonts may look nicer, they'll invariably be harder to read. Remember, people aren't interested in playing games by trying to decipher bizarre typefaces. They just want to know if they should bother reading, and if they like what they read, what they should do. Don't make things confusing; it'll only obscure your message. Avoid being an artist. Be a business-person.

Envelope: There's mixed opinion on whether you should write anything on the envelope. People will open anything in a plain white envelope with their name on it, as it could be a bill, a notice from the government, or a check. Who knows? If you put a headline or message on the outside of the envelope, you run the risk of people dismissing it before even opening it. For example, if you received a letter that said "Inside ... your chance to buy a new Ford Falcon at half the price," you'd be able to instantly decide whether you needed to read the letter or not. You'll find templates and examples of invitation letters in the next section. These will help you get started right away.

One important point. Don't be afraid to deviate from the templates and write your own letter. If you follow the guidelines above, there's no reason why you can't write a letter that works just as well (or much better) than the template letters.

Step 5: How Do You Get the Most Out of the Sale?

It's one thing to attract hundreds of people to your closed-door sale, but quite another to actually get them to buy.

I remember one closed-door sale that attracted more people than I've ever seen at one sale. There were probably 500 people lined up at the door of this tiny retail store. Actually, "lined up" is a misnomer. These people were actually struggling for position. At one point, I was certain something was going to break. I was actually working as a counter assistant at the time, so I was more than a little concerned. Anyway, it all started when the boss had this crazy idea. He decided to leave the price tags off all the items of stock, and give each of us a price list. The idea was simple. People would have to ask what the price was, giving us a chance to *sell* the customer. That was a great idea in theory, but I think the boss expected about 50 people to turn up, not 500 hyped-up bargain hunters. There was no way the 3 of us could answer 500 questions all at once.

The sale was a disaster. People came in expecting to see the prices, and then got totally sick of waiting to ask someone. Most looked around, tried in vain to get the attention of a team member, and then went home. Very few really even got the chance to buy.

This illustrates why you need to plan ahead. Give real thought to the sale, and leave nothing to chance. If you don't make the best of it, customers will go home without even opening their wallets.

Here are some things to consider:

Team: Make sure your team fully understands the strategy you've implemented. It's important they understand the vital role they are to play in this strategy. And also, try to give them a rest before the sale starts. There's no point working them all day so that they're too tired to give their best when the sale starts.

Snacks: Provide drinks and a couple of snacks for your customers. This will encourage them to stay longer.

Security: Most sales don't attract hundreds of frenzied people, but some do. In this case, you might need a security officer to help keep control (and also to watch for shoplifters).

"Now its your turn to get something down on paper, Charlie. I want you to draft a letter to customers inviting them to a closed-door sale. Give it a try, will you?"

"Sure. Give me a few moments while I draft something."

Charlie was enthusiastic about this exercise and it wasn't long before he slid the letter across for me to evaluate.

"Great work, Charlie. This is terrific. You've done well."

This is what he produced:

Here's your invitation to the Charlie's Garage's Closed-Door Super Sale!

- Everything slashed
- Bargain package deals
- Giveaways (including a 20-inch Panasonic TV)
- Drinks and snacks
- Past customers ONLY

Good morning, [NAME]:

Charlie's Garage is having its first ever closed-door sale. This is your opportunity to pick up some real bargains.

Here are a few examples:

- Car radios from $19, save $100
- Top-quality synthetic oil from $20, save $30
- Performance tires from $170, save $99

- Major services from $79, save $140
- Dynatunes from $89, save $200

In addition to the bargains, there are a couple of other reasons to attend.

We're giving away a TV—a 20-inch Panasonic (value $699). You simply drop your name into our barrel and you could win. We'll notify the lucky customer by mail.

Also, you'll be able to pick up your VIP card on the night. Every time you have your car serviced you get a stamp. Once you get five stamps, Charlie's Garage pays for you and your partner to have a night on the town. You'll dine at a great restaurant and have a couple of drinks as well.

And on top of that, we'll then upgrade you to a Gold Card member. That means you get all this:

- Free rally jacket on any purchase over $300.
- First option on specials and new products.
- Regular vouchers and discounts from local businesses.
- A dinner for 2 after you've used your card 5 times.
- Coffee or tea every time you visit the garage.
- Gold Member Prices. Or put simply—the very best service on auto accessories.

But first, you need to come in and pick up your VIP card. To collect it, just come along to the closed-door sale and drop the entry form into the barrel (this also automatically enters you into the draw for the TV).

You'll notice I've included 3 forms—one for you and 2 for your friends (they must live at a different address).

Someone will call in the next few days to see if you can make it. If not, why not phone ahead and ask to see the bargains before the sale? But remember, this sale is only open to yourself and 2 of your friends. If you'd like to bring more than 2 people, please call to make a special arrangement.

I look forward to seeing you there.

Charlie

Charlie's Garage

P.S. Remember, the dinner-for-2 voucher is yours after you get 5 stamps on your VIP card. Bring this letter and you'll get the first stamp automatically. Make a purchase on the night and you'll immediately get another one. That's 2 stamps towards becoming a Gold Club Member.

Examples

Announcing . . . a very special diamond promotion open only to very special customers.

Dear [name],

For the first time ever, Jolissa's Jewellers is holding a closed door sale—a one-time, not-to-be-repeated opportunity on October 22nd. This is strictly for preferred customers and NOT open to the public.

The sale begins at 7:00 p.m. and ends when the last customer leaves.

Through fortunate purchase agreements with diamond merchants, I have secured a range of diamonds for previously unimagined prices. I am able to offer these to you for far less than retail—approximately 65 percent less in many cases.

I am unable to publish these prices, as my competitors would be seriously distressed.

In addition, every item in the store will be open to negotiation, and all reasonable offers will be accepted. This is your only opportunity to buy jewellery at prices my competitors would gag at.

I look forward to seeing you there. Please RSVP by the 15th of October.

Brian Davis
Jolissa Jewellers

P.S. You are entitled to bring along one friend who is not a regular Jolissa Jewellers customer. But only one.

Your invitation to the Mt. Eden Motorcycles closed-door sale.

- Up to 75 percent off all stock
- Great deals on a complete range of never-been-seen before stock—jackets, helmets, gloves
- Food and drinks
- New and classic bikes on show
- Lucky door prize—a $495 HJC helmet

Dear [name],

I wanted to write and tell you about our closed-door sale—a one-time, not-to-be-repeated event exclusively for valued Mt. Eden Motorcycles customers.

Here are the reasons to make sure you're there:

- Stock reduced to clear
- Completely new stock at prices that will NOT be available to the public
- Food and drinks
- 7 super-hot bikes on display
- An awesome lucky door prize

And that's just the start! It's also your chance to mix with 200 other bike enthusiasts.

So whether you're a dirt rampager or a road demon, make your way to Mt. Eden Motorcycles and score a great deal. I suggest you bring your credit card, checkbook, and a loan from your mother. It's going to be a great night.

Here are the details:

What: The Mt. Eden Motorcycles Closed-Door Sale

Who: YOU and 200 other enthusiastic bike riders

When: 7:00-11:00 p.m., 21st October

Where: Mt. Eden Motorcycles

Why: Reread this letter!

I look forward to seeing you there.

Lisa Davies
Mt. Eden Motorcycles

P.S. You may bring one other person, but only ONE—absolutely no exceptions. This sale is exclusively for loyal customers of Mt. Eden Motorcycles.

You're Invited!

The first Longboard Revolution Surfing Day

Dear [name],

Before I go any further, I'd like to say thanks—thanks for supporting Longboard Revolution. Whether you surf just for the fun of it or competitively, we'd like to think our store caters to YOU.

With gratitude in mind, I've organized something special for my top 200 customers—a surfing day. Here's what we have planned:

- An all-you-can-eat breakfast on the beach. For just $5 a head, you can fill up on bacon, eggs, cereal, toast, and juice.
- A 45-minute talk, "How to catch a great wave and stay on it, every time" . . . I've spoken to so many surfers in my 12 years out on a board, and they always ask how I do what I do. I've condensed the best tips into one short lesson. This is free, and will happen right after breakfast.
- A showing of the latest boards and accessories. I'll be showing my new boards, and we'll be getting reps along from Billabong, Rusty, Rip Curl, and more.
- Great deals on everything in store. Straight after the product demos, we'll all go back to the store. There will be special "guest-only" prices on everything. If you're after a new wetsuit or new board, this will be the day to buy it.

- Tides check and recommendation. I've been surfing the coast for 12 years and have a knack for picking where the good surf will be. If you're up for the bigger waves, you can come with me. If you're more a beginner, I'll be recommending good spots for you.
- A day of surfing—and not just a normal day. You'll be armed with a bunch of new skills, and you'll be surfing with ME. You'll make some new friends and have a great time.
- After-surf relaxation. Naturally, all that surfing can make you thirsty, so we'll be heading back to my favorite watering hole for a beer. The perfect end to the perfect day.
- The chance to become one of the first members of the Longboard Club. We're starting up a special club designed for people who love to surf. Whether you're a weekend surfer or a religious once-a-day beach bum, you'll want to become a member. I'll explain more on the day.

The best part is this. It's all FREE! All you have to pay for is your breakfast (only $5 for all you can eat), plus any drinks. So make sure you're there. The details are [details].

You must RSVP on [telephone number] before [date].

I look forward to seeing you there,

Nigel Beckham

Longboard Revolution

P.S. There is one catch. To come, you need to bring a friend. And this friend must be a person who has never been to Longboard Revolution before. If you have a friend who has been to our store, and is also planning to come, you must BOTH bring someone new. See, we'd like to introduce our store to as many surfers as we can. Inviting your friends is a great way to do just that.

Part 3

Loyalty Strategies

"Encouraging your existing customers to return is one of the most important things you can do, Charlie. You see, until they've bought from you an average of two times, you're losing money. That's because your acquisition costs are high. But get them to come back more often and they'll not only become profitable, they'll become loyal customers, moving up the Loyalty Ladder on their way to being a Raving Fan. I'll talk more about this later."

Customer loyalty is such an important topic, and I wanted to spend time discussing it with Charlie. You see, it's far easier *keeping* a customer than *finding* a new one. Yet most businesses seem determined to do it the hard way, chasing prospects that may never become customers.

"Most of my customers seem loyal, Brad. I do enjoy a very high level of repeat business. Take you, for example."

"Yes, I'm sure you do, Charlie. But the fact is, unless you actively do things to encourage your customers to keep doing business with you, there's always the chance they may be lured away by another garage, isn't there? And furthermore, by concentrating on loyalty strategies, you'll be increasing their average dollar sale and their number of transactions at the same time. This will have a direct impact on your bottom line."

This is something most businesses miss. They fail to realize there are five, and only five, basic areas to concentrate on when trying to influence the bottom line. They are leads, conversion rate, number of transactions, average dollar sale, and margins. Nothing more. And working *with* existing customers has got to be *cheaper* and *easier* than fishing for new ones.

"Let me outline some powerful strategies I've introduced to hundreds of business all over the world, Charlie. They're easy to implement and they work. And don't forget to take notes. You'll find them useful when it comes time to design your own loyalty strategies."

Charlie sat back and listened intently as I continued. Here follows a detailed explanation of successful loyalty strategies that could work for your business too.

After reading the next few paragraphs, jump straight in and start going through The Six Steps to Creating a Successful Loyalty Strategy. Each step covers an important aspect of loyalty campaigns. These are things that you must give careful consideration to. Each step represents the cornerstone of a great strategy.

Make sure you make notes as you go. When you come to write your first few strategies, you'll need to refer back to these scribblings.

Refer back to Part 1 and reread the section on Offers. This is important when it comes to developing loyalty strategies.

You'll also find great examples of loyalty campaign letters, some of which may apply directly to your business. And you'll find templates of successful loyalty strategies.

This means you can combine your new knowledge into a format you can be confident will bring results. All you need to do is fill in the gaps. That's how easy it is.

But remember, it's vital you test and measure as you go. You see, while there are certain rules to marketing successfully, it's still largely a matter of trial and error. This makes it essential that you meticulously record every result. It's extra work, but you'll be glad when you have a marketing strategy that you know will produce results. That confidence only comes from testing and measuring. Read about Testing and Measuring in more detail toward the end of this book.

What Is a Successful Loyalty Strategy?

The expectations of novice business owners tend to be unrealistic. They expect that 80 percent of people will adopt their loyalty system and go bananas over it. The truth is, most loyalty strategies will never get anywhere near that response.

Does This Make Them Unsuccessful?

No. If you are getting people to come back more often than they were planning to, and the extra profits more than cover the total cost of promoting, and running, the campaign, it has been successful.

In more simple language, if it's making you money, it works.

For example, let's say it costs you $250 to mail a loyalty card to every one of your customers. The deal is, every sixth purchase is free. Now let's imagine that you get 50 customers (out of 150) who start using their card regularly. It's a bit complex, but if you sit down and spend some time thinking about it, you can work out whether the strategy is increasing your profits. Remember, if your loyalty card is only being used by people who would have come back regularly without an incentive, you're really just giving away free stuff.

That's something you need to watch out for. You may notice that your best customers go mad with the loyalty card, acclaiming it as your best idea ever.

Remember, they would be dealing with you anyway.

A successful strategy will bring back people who like you but aren't dealing with you regularly, or the people who float from one business to the next.

What Makes a Successful Loyalty Strategy?

Remember, you want your strategy to be strong enough to pull in the "swing voters"—the people who don't really care where they buy from, or who feel equally loyal to two or more outlets.

There are a number of factors that determine the success or failure of any loyalty strategy. They include:

Offer: Success is reliant upon how strong your offer is. For example, every sixth meal free, or every sixth haircut free will probably be strong enough to keep people coming back. On the other hand, 10 percent off your 10th purchase is probably not. It needs to be appealing enough for people to say, "Wow, that's a good deal. I'll remember that."

Satisfaction: People need to be happy with your service to begin with. If they were not satisfied with their first interaction with you, it's unlikely they'll come back anyway. It may sound obvious, but it's a reminder to get the little things right before worrying about a loyalty campaign.

Convenience: If people find it easy to keep the loyalty card handy, there is a better chance they will use it. If, for example, it's too big to fit into their wallet, they'll probably throw it away.

Promotion and Exposure: If you treat your loyalty card like it's nothing special, your customers will too. Ask them every time they buy, "Do you have your loyalty card handy?" Make sure that every person who comes in knows it's available and is offered one.

These issues and more are covered in depth in the next section.

The Six Steps to Creating a Successful Loyalty Strategy

Step 1: Why Use a Loyalty System?

Before doing anything, you need to work out whether a loyalty strategy is the right thing for your business.

Let's look at your business in a little more depth. For a loyalty card to work, your business should ideally have:

Frequently Purchased Product: Hairdressers, restaurants, and groceries are all excellent examples. On the other hand, real estate agents and car dealers are examples of businesses that will struggle with a loyalty campaign. For them it's usually so long "between drinks" that people will forget who you are. There are things they can do to remind them, but a loyalty card will be all but meaningless. You can't expect people to hold onto it for 25 years.

Floating Customers: If your customers are already loyal, there's no real point in offering them anything else. You may want to send them a gift, or a thank-you card occasionally, but offering them every xth purchase free is unnecessary. A loyalty card system is good if you see customers come in once, then not again, or if they seem to drop back in every year when you know they would have to buy your product or service at least six times in between.

Margins to Play With: If you went by the above criteria alone, it would seem that gas stations are ideal for a loyalty system. They have a frequently purchased product and floating customer base. The fact is, there is no margin in gas, and as a result, no chance of offering anything worthwhile. They could offer $1 off every 10th purchase of fuel, but who would care? You need healthy margins so that you can offer something attractive.

A Good Product or Service: If your product or service is flawed, you'll do more to damage your reputation than enhance it. Added to that, people would not use your loyalty system. They'll try you once, and then leave you for someone who can deliver what they promise. Improve your quality first, and then worry about getting your customers back.

Step 2: Who Is Your Target Market?

Before you even buy the envelopes for your campaign, you need to identify exactly whom it is you're trying to reach. Precisely who is your target market?

A failure to answer this question will cost you hundreds in wasted dollars and lead to a poor conversion rate. To avoid costly mistakes, you need to know who your potential customers are before you start mailing letters out to them.

Knowing your target market will also enable you to write in a way that your prospects will relate to. Using terms and phrases that are commonly used by them will greatly increase the effectiveness of your letters.

So let's get specific. Who are the people most likely to be interested in your product or service. Here are some guidelines:

Age: How old are they?

Sex: Are they male or female?

Income: How much do they make?

Where do they live?: Are they local, or do they come from miles around to deal with you?

Step 3: What Can You Offer Them?

If you really want your loyalty system to work, you need to do two things:

1. Do everything you can to improve your product or service. Give the best quality you can for the price you are selling for, and take the time to improve your service. Build rapport and be genuinely interested in what the customer wants. This is the best way to ever build loyalty.

2. Work out what you can offer the customers in return for their loyalty. This will give them a feeling of being part of something special, and let them know they are valued. It also gives them the idea that they are "spoken for." For example, imagine a florist that offers a free carnation, sent to anyone in the local area, every time a VIP member orders. When another florist comes along making offers, the customers will block them out—they already "belong" to a florist.

OK, so how do you work out what you can offer your customers? It has to be appealing and generous, yet must not cut heavily into your profit margin.

For some businesses, that's going to be tough. There is just so little margin in some product or service types that it's almost impossible to find some leeway.

Here is a list of options:

- **A free service or product.** Work out the hard cost on your product or service. How many times would the customers have to buy before you could warrant giving them the product or service for free?
- **Free delivery.** How much would it cost you to deliver the product free of charge? Work out the cost against your profit margin and the lifetime value of your customer.
- **Something extra with every sale.** Find a small item (like a chocolate or a consumable accessory) and throw it in with every sale. Again, you need to work out the cost against your margins. This can be a good way to introduce customers to other items in your product range.
- **A free service with another noncompetitive business.** In many cases, you'll get this free. The other business could offer a free service in order to tap into your customer base.
- **Use a lucky draw system.** To determine the value of the lucky draw items, do the following. Work out how much profit you'll make from 100 sales. Now decide how much of that profit you can afford to put back into your loyalty system. Divide that figure by 100. You now have the approximate value of each lucky draw item.

- **Give your customers the VIP treatment.** Perhaps they'll receive complimentary muffins and coffee while they wait, plus any magazine of their choice.

It's important that you know your margins and how much you're willing to sacrifice in order to get your loyalty club up and running. Once you know how much you can spend on customers each time they buy, you can start making some realistic decisions.

Here's an example. Let's say you service cars. The average price of a service is $95, $38 of which is profit. Now, every time a customer chooses to have his car serviced with you, he is giving you $38 (for the sake of simplicity, we won't worry about other costs for now).

Now the question is, how much are you willing to pay for customer loyalty? To answer this, you need to work out how much of a problem it really is. Be honest. Do most customers come and see you once, then never return, or do they always return? If they come in once then take off, you have to ask yourself what are you doing to drive them away?

It may be that you are doing everything right. Perhaps it's just that they don't see anything special about you. They see no reason to come back to you in preference to anyone else.

This is where a loyalty club comes into play.

Remember, a good customer for life is worth more than just the total amount they spend. During the course of one year, how many friends will customers recommend you to? The average business sees about two referrals every year from each customer. For each $38 they give you, why not give them $7 back? You can do a lot with that $7. You could give them a free tire cleaning with every service, plus a piece of cake and a coffee while they wait. You could also fill their cars with scents of their choice and give their cars a quick vacuum.

And that's on top of all the great stuff you do already—free pickup and delivery, a complete written report with a "plain English" explanation and a 3-month guarantee. Plus, you're friendly, clean, and a little more sophisticated than the average mechanical workshop.

Now if you had a mechanic who did all that for you, would you become a loyal customer? You bet! You'd say to your friends, "Every time I go to my mechanic, he gives me the most delicious chocolate cake and a cappuccino. And he asks me how I want my car to smell. He's got this special aromatherapy stuff that makes it smell like a pine forest. Oh yeah, and he's a good mechanic, too."

Think about the actual cost of going the extra mile in this way. You could bake two cakes at the start of the day and buy a cappuccino machine. You've just created something special you can do for your customers, not to mention a real point of uniqueness.

Of course, many mechanics have a "Cafe Bar" where you make your own coffee in a plastic cup, but how many serve you a piece of delicious cake and a cappuccino in a real cup?

This is a perfect example of a small and cheap way to make your customers feel like they are part of a club.

Now what can you do? How much of your profit are you willing to give back in exchange for your customer's eternal loyalty?

Once you know that, you are ready for the next question—what to spend that money on?

Step 4: How Do You Create a System That Works?

By now you'll have worked out one thing—that loyalty is worth paying for. A good customer will not only bring you income, but also stacks of referrals. Once customers "commit" to a business, they have no problem sending in their friends.

You will also have worked out that loyalty systems are not right for every business. If your customers are already loyal, you'd be better off just sending them a small gift or thank-you card every now and again.

If your customers mostly come to you once and then are never seen again, you have to give some real thought to the quality of your product and service. People are "once bitten, twice shy." If you burn them once, all the loyalty cards and incentives in the world will probably not bring them back.

The best opportunity for a loyalty system is when you have customers who are happy with your service but feel pretty indifferent about it. They were satisfied with their experience with you but don't feel there's any reason to choose you over any of your competitors.

They don't know it, but these floating customers are waiting for someone to "claim" them. If a business actually puts its hand out and says, "We'll take you," it would probably win the customer's business for life.

A loyalty card system is a perfect way to claim customers. It's also a good way to say to the customer, "We like having you as a customer. We'd like to see you back."

People are often surprised when you tell them about your loyalty system. They expect just to float in, get what they need, then float out again. Suddenly, you're saying to them, "Hey, you, we want you as a customer. That means commitment—a monogamous relationship."

People are usually a little taken aback. "I didn't think you even noticed me here," they think. That's unfortunately how it is. Most customers feel unnoticed. They're just another number. A loyalty card has the benefit of making them feel special.

Now, before we go on to examine the elements of a powerful loyalty club system, let's cover the main reasons why loyalty systems fail:

- **The team doesn't promote it.** You've seen it all before. Business owners stick a sign up on the wall that says, "Ask about our loyalty club." Surprisingly, nobody ever does. There's no reason to. The team members do not have to put themselves out at all—if anyone wants to join the loyalty club, they'll ask, right? Wrong! The team has to get behind the idea, and mention it to every customer. You have to embark on a membership drive.

- **The offer is not generous enough.** The critical point is when you hand customers their VIP cards and explain the benefits to them. If they see the benefit, they'll put them in their wallets and make a mental note to use them next time. If they don't, they'll look for the nearest bin and wonder if you have mental problems. As mentioned before, you need to work out how much you're willing to spend to win your customers' loyalty. If you can't offer something appealing, you may be better off leaving the idea alone altogether.

- **There is no follow-up.** If you simply give customers loyalty cards and never mention it again, they'll forget all about it. You have to ask customers whether they are members of your VIP Club. If they say no, explain to them why they should be. If they say yes, say, "Great, let me stamp your card," then remind them of the benefits. Remember, people are just animals. They need to be trained. You need to give positive reinforcement every time they do what you want them to. If a customer brings in a card, say "Great, you're almost up to your free service," or "Hey, you've only got three more meals to go before you get that special ice cream cake."

Now that you know what doesn't work, let's look at what does.

Most importantly, people have to see the benefit in presenting their cards. They have to feel like they're working towards something, or alternately getting special privileges that everyone else is missing out on. That makes them feel smart, and like they've got one up on everybody else.

That leads to the two basic types of loyalty systems:

1. Customers get a benefit after spending $x, or visiting x times.

2. Customers get a benefit every time.

So how do you work your loyalty system? Here are a variety of different ways:

- **Every sixth service free:** This is ideal for mechanics, hairdressers, restaurants, or any business where customers have to come back regularly. The way it works is simple. You give the customer a card. She gets it stamped each time she visits. On her sixth visit, the meal, service, or product is free. The effectiveness of this depends on how frequently she visits, and the value of the free item. People will only get involved if the offer seems generous. Offering every tenth purchase free is usually stretching it. The goal is too far out for people to really imagine. If you have a high profit margin, why not go all out and offer every fourth service free? You'll be unbeatable.

- **Credit dollar system:** A customer is given a card. When he presents his card, he receives credit dollars for his purchase. You could do it like this: every $10 he spends earns him 1 credit dollar, which he can spend any time in the future. Of course, you don't give him cash; you give him a specially printed dollar. He'll keep it in his wallet and use it next time. It will also serve as a reminder of your business every time he opens his wallet.
- **Points system:** Every time customers spend, they accumulate points. For example, $10 may equal 100 points. When customers reach a certain number of points, they can spend them on something you sell. They may conserve their points and use them towards something better. You could have a range of "prizes." Look at the Frequent Flyer system. Unquestionably, the rewards are so minuscule you'd have to spend a zillion dollars even to get on a plane, but people love the idea. They feel as though they are working towards something.
- **Extra service perks:** Take our example of the mechanic. Each time customers come in, they get extra stuff—cake, cappuccino, special-smelling oils for their cars, free magazines to read. Work out what special extras you could provide for your customers. This can also help stimulate referrals and get people talking. Do things that really get people excited. Here's a good example for a hairdresser: While a customer is waiting for her hair to change color, why not offer to go and do some shopping for her? If she needs a paper and some milk, offer to go and get it! Or why not ask her to fill out a sheet that asks about her favorite music or movies. You could have her favorite song playing when she next arrives. Or you could have her favorite movie showing. Wouldn't that be sensational? Depending on your profit margin, these ideas are certainly possible.
- **Send gifts and thank-you cards:** This is a good one if your profit margin is low, your customers are already loyal, or you only see them every couple of years or so. Why not send them newsletters, thank-you cards, and the occasional gift? Books make fantastic gifts. You can go to the publisher and say you'd like to buy 1000, and you want a special rate. ***You can even find out-of-print books and arrange the rights so that you can print them yourself.*** A book shows real thought and helps build rapport. You can

write a letter than says, "I read this book and thought it was great. I'm sure you'll enjoy it too."

So once you've decided upon the loyalty system that you believe will work best for you, you now have to decide how to promote it to your customers.

Here are some ways:

- A letter: Writing your customers letters is a great way to tell them anything. It lets them know that you have their names and addresses, which in some ways makes them feel special. Also, you get to write down the benefits of being in the loyalty club and promote it in exactly the same way to all your customers. Letters have one advantage over personal contact: When you're speaking personally to a customer and telling him about the loyalty club, you'll find yourself getting bored. You may also forget something, or occasionally not have the time to explain it properly. A letter solves these problems. You do it all at once, and in exactly the same way with every customer. Of course, it does mean that you need an up-to-date customer list. You'll find some examples at the end of this section. But remember this: It's a common misconception that you have to be a great writer to write a letter that works. If your loyalty club is simple and appealing, it doesn't matter how you get the message across.

  Here are some basic guidelines:

  Be brief: Remember, the one sin you don't want to commit when writing a letter is getting off the point, or rambling on too long. If every word and every sentence says something important for the sale, fine. If your letter is full of guff, people will lose interest very quickly. The same applies if you stray from your initial intention and message.

  Your headline: Tell people exactly what they will get from reading the letter. With your loyalty club letter, it should be simple. You could just say, "Now that you're a member of our VIP club, you'll get all of this." Then list the benefits. Or alternately, something like, "Good news!" These headlines have already been proven to work well. Try coming up with your own. Just make it simple, and ensure it expresses a benefit.

Create a strong introduction: The first couple of sentences are important. They tell people whether they should read on in depth or start skimming. Get right to the details of your loyalty club. Let people know right away that this is a letter that's *giving* them something. Include a strong, specific, call to action. If you don't tell them what to do, they probably won't do anything. Give them precise instructions. For example, "Put this card in your wallet now, and make sure you present it next time you come to dine with us." It may be an idea to put a time limit on it too. "This card needs to be used in the next 28 days." Be careful, though. A time limit may be perceived as being too pushy in some cases. You be the judge.

Include concise body copy: The body copy is the actual text between the introduction and the call to action. You don't need to be a great writer to do this part well; it's more important that you get the point across clearly, in as few words as possible, and in logical order. After you write your first draft, go through and edit viciously. Cut out any sentence or word that doesn't need to be there. Next, read it aloud and make sure it flows. Then have a couple of people check through it, and ask them to tell you what they understood from it.

Use a P.S.: One of the most important aspects of the copy is the P.S. In fact, it's often the most read part of the letter. It pays to include a major point right at the end. For example, an extra special bonus if they use the loyalty card within the next couple of days. People tend to read the P.S. because it's unexpected. They are surprised that someone has forgotten to include something. Some professional copywriters use up to four P.S.'s and write up to half a page for each. It sounds crazy, but it seems to work.

Make the layout "fun": When writing your letter, forget everything you learned at school about writing business letters. Indent paragraphs, splash bold throughout, use bullet points, and give everything lots of space. If you look at your letter and think to yourself, "My god, that's a lot," you'll need to take another look at the layout. Perhaps it needs to be spread out. Or maybe you need to take a paragraph and put the main points next to bullets.

Watch out for letters that are too long or too short: The number of pages is less important than the actual layout. If spacing it out spills the letter onto three pages rather than one, that's OK, just as long as it looks fun to read. There's a common perception that a one-page letter will always be read. That's not strictly true. If the letter is packed solid with text just so that it'll fit on one page, people will be more turned off than if it were four pages and spaced.

Avoid anything that's hard to read: Type your letter in a standard font: Times New Roman or Courier. While another more artistic font may look nicer, it'll be harder to read. Remember, people aren't interested in deciphering typefaces; they just want to know if they should bother reading on, and if they like what they read, what they should do.

- **Follow up with a phone call:** If you mail your customers a letter, then call soon after. You'll be surprised by the leap in response you get. People have the chance to ask you questions, and this will help cement your relationship.

- **Face to face:** Telling people about your loyalty club can work well. It gives the customer a feeling that they've been chosen. There's no better time than after you've been speaking for a while, and you seem to have developed a little rapport. It's almost like when you were speaking to a member of the opposite sex and they said, "By the way, do you have my phone number?" or "Have you heard about my party?" You feel as though you've been so charming and witty that you've just been accepted into a club.

  Of course, the opportunities to create such moments are rare. Usually, it's a little less magical, but that shouldn't stop you from introducing people to your loyalty club.

  Just ask them if they are a member of your loyalty club, or even better, try this: "I've seen you in here many times. You're a member of our loyalty club, aren't you?" They'll then say no and look confused. You could then lead on with (using a restaurant as an example), "But you know that every sixth meal is free, and you get priority seating, plus a 15-minute guarantee on every meal, don't you?" They'll again say no and feel like they've been left out. You can then say, "Well, let's fix that right now. Let me get your details and give you your VIP card immediately." When he tells you his name, there's nothing wrong with saying something like, "Robert ... that's right, I thought it was, but couldn't quite remember." That gives the customer the impression you've been noticing him, which again will make him feel special.

Once you've gotten their details and given them the card, run them through the benefits of being a member. Every time they come in, make sure you ask them whether they have their card with them. You need to train them. Soon it will become habit.

- **In-store flyer:** If you have plenty of customers or are usually too busy to sit down and introduce every customer to the club personally, a flyer can do the job for you. Just create a small flyer that explains the benefits of being part of the VIP club. When the customer has finished buying whatever she is buying, just say, "You're a member of our VIP club, aren't you?" She'll say, "No, what on earth are you talking about?" Hand her the flyer and say, "Just read this. I think you'll like it."
- **Phone:** Instead of mailing your customers a letter, why not phone them directly and explain the loyalty card? This method will work best when you only have a small number of customers and you have good relationships with them. If you have 2000 customers who barely know you, you'll find it pretty hard going calling them all cold. This is best for service businesses that work one-on-one with each customer.

Step 5: When to Introduce People to the Loyalty Strategy

Once you've worked out what you're prepared to give your customers in exchange for their loyalty, you need to work out when the ideal time is to introduce them to your loyalty system.

In some cases, you need to do it on their first visit. This needs to be done delicately. You can't really say, "I know this is the first time I've seen you, but I think of you as one of our most important customers." People will see right through that.

If you're going to hit people with the idea right away, it has to be more a "regular customer card" or "frequent buyers rewards program."

If you have a suspicion that many of your customers come to you once, find out that you don't do anything special, and then leave you for someone else, you need to get them straight away.

If you get people coming back pretty regularly anyway, it may be worth delaying the card until later. Then it can be called a VIP Card or a Special Customer Card. It will have the impact of encouraging them to come back more often.

Step 6: What Else Do You Need to Think About?

Use this section as a final checklist. Once you're happy with your loyalty strategy, run through and make sure you're ready to get started. Here are a few things you may not have thought of:

Team Training: Does your team fully understand the strategy you've implemented? It's important that they understand the vital role they are to play in it.

Check Stock and Team Levels: It's unlikely your loyalty campaign will bring in hundreds of extra sales (very few actually do), but you need to be prepared for a sizable response. There would be nothing worse than having a rush of extra sales only to find you have no stock or are too busy to take advantage it.

"What do you think, Charlie? Can you write to your customers announcing your VIP Club?"

"Yes, I sure can, Brad. Give me five minutes and I'll hand you a draft."

This is what he wrote:

Here's what you get when you're a Charlie's Garage VIP Card holder:

- A special gift every time you have your car serviced—five liters of the best-grade synthetic oil or a dinner for 2.
- A special surprise on your fifth service.

- The best service and advice.
- Below-cost service.

Good morning, [NAME]:

Thanks for allowing Charlie's Garage to service your car.

Your decision to come to us tells me you value quality—and that your number-one concern is how well your car performs. That's what we are concerned about too, and why we confidently give our personal seal of approval to everything we do.

As a small token of my appreciation, I've sent you a special Charlie's Garage VIP card. As mentioned above, it entitles you to bonuses just for dealing with us. You'll notice I've also included two extra cards. These are for your friends. Please pass them on.

Thanks, [NAME], and we look forward to speaking with you soon,

Charlie

Charlie's Garage

P.S. To become a member of the VIP club, you just need to call up and claim a gift I've arranged for you—a FREE 1-liter can of oil (you don't even need to make a purchase!). Likewise, your friends are entitled to the same gift. Once they collect it, their cards will be validated. Do this today. Please call first.

Examples

Example 1

Here's some fantastic news from Eaton's Florist—

How to save on your florist fees:

Good morning, [NAME]:

Before I let you in on the good news, let me just say thanks. It's been a pleasure supplying [business name] with flowers, and I hope our association blossoms (if you'll pardon the pun) into a long one.

But here's why I'm writing to you:

From this point onwards, every purchase you make with Eaton's Florist earns you 10 percent credit dollars. For example, if you spend $100, you'll receive $10 worth of Flower Dollars.

At your current level of spending, you'll earn around $x per month in Flower Dollars. You can use this credit towards anything from Eaton's Florist, and there's no time limit.

And here's the truly exciting part:

You'll notice I've included an envelope with this letter. It contains [number] staff VIP cards. Just give each of your employees one of these cards. I think they'll really appreciate it. Here are three reasons why:

1. They'll be entitled to special VIP delivery. Either the flowers get there within 4 hours of their call, or they're FREE.
2. They get FREE wrapping on any purchase, no matter how small.
3. Every time they spend over $20 on flowers, they'll receive a FREE box of Roses chocolates—the classic combination.

And here's how these staff cards will help YOU:

Every time your employees buy flowers through Eaton's, you'll receive 10 percent of their purchases as credit dollars.

Let me illustrate with an example. If someone from your organization buys a bouquet for $45 and flashes her card (or mentions it over the phone), $4.50 is credited to your account.

And this happens every time that person flashes the card (even if she's ceased working with [business name]).

So here's what you need to do:

Simply distribute the cards among your workers. You might want to send a short memo around, explaining what the card is for. If you don't have time, just hand them out. Everything's explained on the back of the card.

And remember, every time you, or one of your employees, makes a purchase, you'll receive 10 percent back in credit dollars. You'll receive an update of your credit dollars every month.

I'll give you a call later today just to make sure everything's crystal clear.

Looking forward to speaking with you then.

Peter Eaton

Eaton's Florist

P.S. Here's some more good news. I've included your last two purchases in the new system. That means you already have $z credit dollars. I'd appreciate it if you could return the favor and hand the cards out to your staff.

All the best,

Example 2

Here are six reasons why life smells sweeter when you're a West Harbor Flowers VIP card member. (It's easy, instant and FREE):

1. Every tenth order FREE (plus an extra gift)
2. Guaranteed delivery in 2 hours
3. Access to a member's only 800 order line
4. Telephone reminders of special occasions
5. Regular exclusive offers
6. A free rose for one person of your choice

Good morning, [NAME]:

You read correctly. All of the above is yours when you choose to become a West Harbor Flowers VIP card holder.

Faster than you can ask, "What's the catch?" I'll tell you up front. There isn't one. See, we'd like you to call us every time you need flowers or gifts, and for that reason, we're making you a very special offer.

When we call you tomorrow, simply give us your details and you'll automatically become a member of our VIP club.

You'll see the benefits almost immediately—starting next week, when we send a person of your choice a FREE rose. After that, you'll get the most incredible service on flowers anywhere in the local area—guaranteed delivery in less than 2 hours, a member's-only free call orders number, regular updates on our latest specials, and more.

And that's not even the best part.

The card included with this letter entitles you to every tenth order free (anything to the value of the average price of your previous nine purchases).

And when you've completed your card, you mail it in for a special gift and entry into our regular mystery weekend competitions (drawn every 2 weeks)—you could end up anywhere in your country.

And even better than that—

West Harbor VIP club members never forget their anniversaries, their best friends' birthdays or Mother's Day. Why? Because we call and remind you every time. If you'd like us to automatically send out their favorite flowers, just dictate a message, and we'll get them out.

And remember—we don't just sell flowers. Choose from a range of balloons, baskets, teddy bears, and gifts. Of course, all of this counts towards your FREE order.

A member of my team will call you tomorrow, run through a couple of questions, and add you to our VIP members list.

Thanks once again, and I look forward to a long and happy association.

Ann-Maree DeVos

West Harbor Flowers

P.S.We keep track of your purchases on computer, meaning you can order over the phone. The card is for your reference. Just mark off a square each time you make a purchase.

P.P.S. Remember, to celebrate your membership, West Harbor Flowers will send a person of your choice a free rose.

Example 3

New from Q-Data—the Q-Club Card.

Good morning, [NAME]:

Thanks for your business. In appreciation, we'd like to make you a Q-Club member. I've sent your card with this letter.

Here's how the system works:

There are five "star" levels. Each time you move up a level, you'll qualify for just that little bit more. Here's what I mean:

Level 1
Same-Day Delivery
Bimonthly Newsletter

Level 2
First Offer on Specials
Q-Dollars Every Time You Purchase

Level 3
Access to Q-Data Web site
90-Minute Express Metro Delivery
Cross Promotion to Q-Data Clients

Level 4
Biyearly Cocktail Parties
Automatic On-Site Reordering

Level 5
Gifts and Truly Awesome Service

There are particular criteria for each star level. I won't go into that now. I'll leave that for when I phone you later this week.

I've also included a few stickers with your Q-Data number. Stick these on your printers, computers, and scanners—just as a reminder to use your card.

I'll give you a call in the next few days, just to check that you've received, and understood, this letter. I'll also let you know what star level you are now, and what you can do to reach the next one.

Look forward to speaking with you soon.

Michael McKergow
Q-Data

P.S. When we speak, I'll also be asking for the names of a couple of people you think would also like to be Q-Club members. I'm not offering this to new customers—only loyal current customers and their associates.

Example 4

Here's how to get one of these five classic books FREE . . .

Hi there . . .

Before I say any more, let me simply say thanks for your purchase with Zen Gallery.

Your decision to visit our store tells me that you're interested in making positive changes in your life—and I'm willing to bet that you've got at least two friends with a similar passion.

For that reason, I've included 2 Club Zen cards—each already stamped with a $20 purchase. Give the cards to two people you know would appreciate them. They'll then be well on their way to becoming Gold Card members.

Of course, you'll also be introducing them to the city's premier personal growth store, a favor I'm certain they'll thank you for.

And that's not all. When your two friends bring their cards in and make any purchase over $5, I'll happily send you a small gift—a book of your choice from the selection above. This is simply a token of my appreciation, and in keeping with one of my favorite sayings, "The man who shares knowledge freely will always be rewarded in the most favorable way."

Thanks once again, and I look forward to seeing you in-store soon,

Garry Heiner
Managing Director—Zen Gallery

P.S. Owing to changing stock, I can only make this offer valid for the next 28 days. Keep these cards in your wallet/purse and pass them on next time you see your friends.

Templates

Template 1

YES, we've made you a [business name] Preferred Customer Card holder.

- [benefit 1]
- [benefit 2]
- [benefit 3]

Good morning, [NAME]:

Thanks for your purchases with [business name].

Your decision to come to us tells me you appreciate good service, and [something else that sets your business apart].

Please accept this VIP card as a token of my appreciation. You get something extra every time you come and a surprise on your [number] purchase. I won't give it away. You'll find out when you get there.

Thanks, [NAME], and I look forward to speaking with you soon,

[Your name]
[Business name]

P.S. This card needs to be used some time in the [time period], and is then valid for [x] years.

Template 2

[Big "six-reasons" headline]

(It's easy, instant, and FREE)

1. Benefit . . .
2. Benefit . . .
3. Benefit . . .
4. Benefit . . .
5. Benefit . . .
6. Benefit . . .

Good morning, NAME:

You read correctly. All of the above is yours when you choose to become a [business name] VIP cardholder.

Faster than you can ask, "What's the catch?" I'll tell you up front. There isn't one. See, we'd like you to call us every time you need [product type], and for that reason, we're making you a very special offer.

When we call you tomorrow, simply give us your details and you'll automatically become a member of our VIP club. You'll see the benefits almost immediately—starting next week, when we [do something special for you]. After that, you'll get the most incredible service on [product] anywhere—benefit 1, benefit 2, benefit 3.

And that's not even the best part.

The card included with this letter entitles you to every tenth order free (anything to the value of the average price of your previous nine purchases).

And when you've completed your card, you mail it in for a special gift and entry into our regular [competition] (drawn fortnightly).

And even better than that—

[more service benefits of being a member]

A member of my team will call you tomorrow, run through a couple of questions, and add you to our VIP members list.

Thanks once again, and I look forward to a long and happy association,

[Your name]

[Business name]

P.S. We keep track of your purchases on computer, meaning you can order over the phone. The card is for your reference. Just mark off a square each time you make a purchase.

Part 4

Worth Considering

"These strategies aren't the only ones you could use to increase your number of transactions, Charlie. But they're the ones I think you need to put in place right away."

I could tell he was feeling a whole lot more confident now that we had been through, in some detail, strategies designed to improve his bottom line. You see, now he actually could understand *how* to go about implementing them in a manner that suits his business, and he understands *why* they work.

"Thanks, Brad. I know I've got more on my plate for the time being, but one thing all this has done is make me more curious about business in general. I mean, I really want to know more. Do all your clients feel this way?"

"Absolutely. This is because they begin to view business as a game. There are rules to play by, and if you understand them and follow them, you'll find you're not being constantly stopped in your tracks as you try to make progress. You know, the referee isn't always blowing his whistle at you. You'll suddenly find you begin reaching your business goals much easier. Your game gets better the more you play."

"And I suppose you begin to have fun," Charlie added with a grin.

"Exactly. Business is supposed to be fun, remember that. But let's explore the similarities between business and sports a little further, shall we?"

I always introduce everyday concepts when trying to explore what many believe to be "dry" business principles.

"If you want to succeed in business, you have to abide by the rules of the game. Every game has rules, and playing the business game is no different."

Charlie nodded.

"So what then do you need to play a game? Any game. Think about this for a minute and jot them down on a sheet of paper."

I noticed his pen was poised above his pad of notepaper.

"Your list will probably look something like this," I continued.

"Rules, playing field, a plan, a team, the opposition, an umpire or referee, goals, a scorekeeper, spectators, a manager, a coach, rewards, sporting equipment, communication."

He wrote as I spoke.

"OK, let's look at this a bit closer, particularly as it applied to the game of business. There are in actual fact, three sets of *rules* you need to play by. These include *The Rules of the Game.* These are the general rules as laid down by the government, local authorities, banks, legal institutions, and local conventions. You have no control over these rules. Then there's *Your Rules of the Game,* which are your overall vision, mission, goals, and objectives that help determine your rules. They will be established according to your overall situation and circumstances, and reflect your *modus operandi,* ethics, morality, wishes, and desires. You set these rules, and you can change them. And lastly, there's *Your Specific Rules for the Specific Game You Are Playing at the Time.* These will vary according to which marketplace you are dealing in at that moment; the economic climate, your short-term objectives, personal considerations like if you're planning on building up your business to sell it or aiming to franchise it, or if you need to generate a quick cashflow. Again, these are your rules and you can change them to suit your situation."

Charlie was smiling broadly now.

"So I do have plenty of freedom in business, Brad? I can still basically operate how I like?"

"Of course you can, Charlie. It's your business after all. All I'm saying is understand the basic rules and play according to them to achieve what you want to from your business. It's really quite simple—if you know how."

"Just like anything in life," he added. I nodded.

"Business is like a playing a game in other respects as well, " I continued.

"In addition to the *rules*, there is the *playing field* (the market you are dealing in), your *team* (those helping you—could be your spouse, your employees, and your lawyer), the *opposition* (those who are trying to prevent you from succeeding), the *umpire* (government or local authority), the *goals* (your aims and objectives), *scores* (if you're not keeping score, why bother playing?), the *learning experience* (the more you play, the better you get), *spectators* (those who cheer you on or criticize your efforts), the *scorekeepers* (your accountant, bookkeeper or auditor), the *rule makers* (could be you, the industry, or the local authority), *rule enforcers* (police), *managers, coaches* (those who get you to achieve something you wouldn't be able to on your own), the *competition* (those who stimulate you to higher levels of achievement), and the *time limit* (when do you stop playing the game?)."

Charlie sat back and whistled.

"Fascinating stuff, Brad. Fascinating."

"But let me talk now about some of the other strategies you could consider for increasing your number of transactions."

He nodded, and I talked on.

"Of course, there are many more strategies you could use to improve your number of transactions. I make use of no fewer than 50—and they're all tried-and-tested winners. This area of business is vitally important to your overall performance, yet it's one few acknowledge."

Now, dear reader, slide in and take Charlie's place. What follows is general in nature and very adaptable. Once you've made contact with a prospect and done the "hard yards" converting them into a customer, the next task facing you is to get them to come back again, and again, and again. You see, it's with them that your future fortune lies—or your ultimate demise.

Shifting your focus to those who currently do business with you has got to be one of the easiest things you can do; and the rewards can be simply staggering. I'm going to mention again something I hammer home to everyone I coach, and that's to know who your customers are. You'll remember it's the first step in all the strategies outlined in detail throughout this book. So, do you know exactly who deals with you? If not, find out now. Start taking down the details of everyone who comes into your store. Collect as many pertinent details as you can. Develop a database.

Now use your existing customers to transform your bottom line. How do you do this? By tapping into your database. Here's how:

- Keep in contact with everyone on your database by regularly sending them letters, brochures, catalogues, newsletters, and invite them to exclusive closed-door sales and offer them membership in a Loyalty Club. Ideally, your contact rate should not be longer than every three months. It could simply be a phone call to thank them for their past business and to offer them a special deal. But make your contact memorable because dealing with you will probably be the last thing on their minds.

- Constantly offer them specials.

The beauty of working on this area of the Business Chassis is that it achieves a few important objectives all at once. Remember the Loyalty Ladder? Well, by getting your customers to come back time and again, you'll be assisting them to climb the rungs of your Loyalty Ladder. And remember too that once they get to the top, they'll be Raving Fans of your business. This is undoubtedly one of the best assets your business could have. Here's what I mean:

You have to move your customers up this ladder, and you need to keep them moving up the ladder all the time. Think of it just like an ordinary ladder. If you were to step up onto the first rung, would you just hang around there for a while before doing something? No, you would want to climb up right away, or get off.

Now, ask yourself why it is you want to build a loyalty ladder for your business. I'd suggest it is because the first sale you make to a customer is made at a loss. Yes, statistics show 9 out of 10 first sales are made at a loss, because there are advertising costs, marketing costs and commissions that first need to be taken into account. If you don't get that customer to come back and buy again, that customer isn't profitable to you.

Let's now take a closer look at the loyalty ladder and what the various stages on it involve:

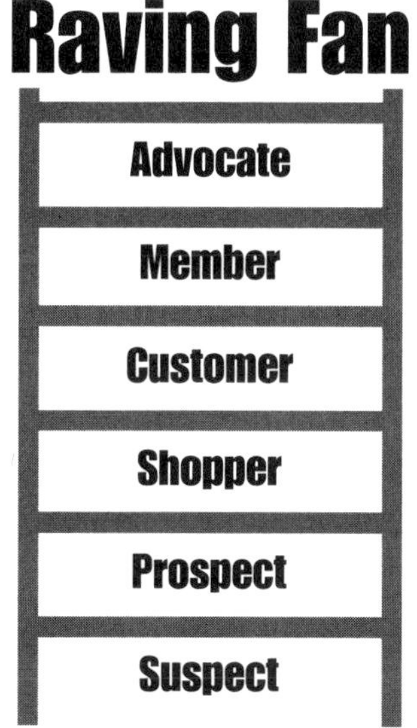

SUSPECT. When they first start out on the loyalty ladder, right at the bottom rung, people are called Suspects. How do you identify them? They are only potential customers at this stage; they fit within your target market and they are willing to buy from you if they are in your geographic area.

PROSPECT. We then move up the ladder to Prospect. A Prospect is a Suspect who has taken some sort of action like phoning in off an ad or visiting your business. You must collect all their details so you can stay in touch. This is most important, as building customer loyalty is all about relationship building. You will be aiming to build a database of Prospects. You now use all your sales skills to move your Prospect one rung up the ladder to the next stage, to that of Customer.

CUSTOMER. To be classified a Customer, your Prospect needs to have spent money, and you need to have recorded the sale in your records. This last step may seem strange, but it is most important, because it allows you to differentiate on your database between Prospects and Customers. You see, if you are planning to send a letter out to all Prospects offering them an incentive to buy, you don't want to be sending it to people who are already Customers. This record will also tell you when they last bought, how often they buy, and what their average dollar sale is.

MEMBER. When your Customers make their second purchase, they become Members. They now have a feeling of belonging. Understand that Customers who make two purchases are 10 times more likely to make more than someone who has only made one. So you need to put some effort into your Members. Give them a membership card and a membership pack. How many of your Customers know all your products? Very few, I would suggest. So why not include a product catalogue in the membership pack? You can also include samples, vouchers, and things like that.

ADVOCATE. Once you have Members, you move them up the ladder to the next level—to that of Advocate. An Advocate is someone who sells you to other people. The criteria for an Advocate are they will give referrals or promote you, and they keep buying. Advocates are one of your major capital assets.

RAVING FAN. Once you have created an Advocate, you need to move them up to the top of the ladder where they become Raving Fans. Understand the difference: an Advocate is someone who will sell for you, whereas a Raving Fan is someone who can't stop selling for you. The exciting thing about Raving Fans is they can almost be regarded as part of your team. They want to see you succeed. Of course, they continue buying from you all along.

Remember, the aim of the game is to move people up from Customer to Raving Fan. This is where you begin to make profit.

Can you now appreciate the importance of concentrating on improving your Number of Transactions?

So what else can you do, in addition to the strategies already discussed in this book?

Here are some areas worth concentrating on:

Customer Service

Customer service is a cliché if ever there was one. And it must be one of the most misconstrued concepts in business today. The name of the game is making customer service *pay*. It never ceases to amaze me how most businesses go about tackling the question of customer service. What most of them do is to start by spending large amounts of money in an attempt to impress their customers. What they fail to do is to find out if this will make them any more money or not. You see, great customer service without bottom-line results is a waste of time and money.

Let me now share with you the three steps you must take to achieving great, and meaningful, customer service.

Step # 1. You must aim for *consistency.* It's no good if whatever you do differs each day. Your customers will want to know that whenever they visit your business, the service will be the same. And it doesn't matter what the level of customer service is, so long as it's consistent. I mean if you are running a five-star hotel you will serve your dinner guests at their tables, whereas if you were running a fast food outlet you wouldn't. This doesn't mean the customer service at the fast food joint is inferior to that at the hotel. It would just be different, at a different level. And you must offer consistency in both service and delivery.

Step #2. Make it *easy* for customers to *buy.* You see, with consistency comes *trust.* By building consistency into your sales process, you will ensure that you systematically surpass their expectations every time they buy from you. They will begin to trust your business; they will know every time they buy from you that there will be no unpleasant surprises. They receive the same pleasant greeting each and every time they arrive, they receive the same efficient and courteous service while they are there, and their questions are answered accurately and honestly. Do everything possible to make their buying experience easy. This way, they will know what to expect when they return next time.

Step #3. Now introduce the *wow* factor. This is the way to create Raving Fans. Understand this: the fundamentals of creating great customer service involve creating a system to make sure your customer's expectations are surpassed, every time. Having satisfied customers implies that you have given them all they've wanted, but nothing more. But if you're going to surpass their expectations, you must systematically go beyond their expectations. Every single day you need to be getting better. To do this, you need to go further than just providing great customer service. You need to implement a customer service plan, which contains the following action points:

- Identify your ideal customers. Find out who they are.
- Create your customer service vision. Remember, customer service is about understanding that the little things are important. You need to make an impression on your customers.

- Conduct market research. You need to ask your ideal customers what they would regard as excellent customer service.
- Now create your customers' customer service vision.
- Take the two visions and combine them to create an ultimate customer service vision.
- Decide what it is you can promise your customers. This must be something you can deliver each and every time. My rule is to underpromise and overdeliver.
- Make sure you get your team involved. Give them the vision, and ask them for ideas on how it can be delivered. Work consistently with them on this.
- Make sure you have continual checkups to ensure you are delivering what you promise.
- As your level of service gets better, move the goalposts. Keep improving.
- Always give your customers more than they expect. I send out free gifts continually.
- And always smile. You see, people love to feel special.

People are willing to *pay* for service—when it's the service they desire. If the service exceeds their expectations, they will *stay* with you and they will *say* good things about your business.

But if your service is poor, they'll *walk* away, they'll *talk* negatively about your business, and they'll *balk* at coming back.

Be consistent, always smile, and give your customers more than they expect. And be sure they leave with a smile on their face.

Most good businesses spend time and money in the pursuit of good customer service so they can get customers to come back and make further purchases. But understand that good customer service in itself isn't any guarantee their Number of Transactions will increase. Take, as an example, two businesses. One gives average customer service and the other prides itself on its good customer service. If the first business writes a follow-up letter to its customers inviting them to shop there again whereas the second one doesn't, where do you think the customers are more likely to shop next? At the first business, even though its customer service is rated as only being average.

You need to concentrate on some other important area of your business to supplement what you're doing on the customer service front. These areas include what you stock (or your Stock in Trade), strategies that affect your sales process, and some strategies that affect the management of your business. Let's go through them individually:

Stock-Related Strategies

How many of your customers actually know what you stock? How many of them know what you sell besides the items they already buy from you? What if they needed something they didn't know you stocked? They'd buy it from someone else, wouldn't they? You'd have just lost a perfect opportunity for increasing that customer's number of transactions.

The frightening thing about this is they'd probably have been more than willing to buy from you because they'd already be comfortable with the way you operate. And by giving your competitor another opportunity of interacting (and impressing) them, you suddenly run the risk of losing this customer altogether because chances are, your competitor also stocks the items this customer already buys from you. How risky is this as a way to run your business?

So what should you do about it?

- Try informing all your customers of your entire range, for starters. Send them an information pack that includes brochures and catalogues. Then become proactive by trying to get them to buy products they don't currently buy from you. Use the opportunity to swing them away from your competitors.

- If you only stock one product people buy regularly, concentrate on expanding your range. Sell accessories or something related to what you currently stock. You'll be pleasantly surprised at how many will buy more from you just because you treated them well the last time they shopped. Write to them or phone them to tell them about your new product range.

- Increase product obsolescence or encourage upgrades. By giving your products a shorter life span, customers will have to upgrade to the newer product. This is a cornerstone of the fashion industry.
- Always have stock. If you don't, you run the risk of losing customers. Understand that customers want two things when dealing with a business; a reasonable deal and reliability.
- Have a product of the week. Offering great deals on a selected product each week is an excellent way of getting people to keep coming back. People love bargains. If you let them know there will be one every week, they'll keep an eye on your business and buy anything that excites them. Remember, this is also an excellent opportunity for staying in touch.

Sales-Related Strategies

The way your sales team goes about interacting with your customers can have a marked effect on your number of transactions. That goes without saying. But have you thought about the following?

- **Preselling or taking prepayments.** Why not get your sales team to sell to customers while they're in the mood to buy? After they've been served in a really impressive way and made their intended purchase, ask them for a deposit on their next purchase. Offer them an incentive to make a down payment. Alternatively, offer a package deal.
- **Contracts.** If this is applicable to the industry you work in, you'll find it's the most potent way of ensuring people return.
- **Till further notice deals.** These can work extremely well, especially if you deal in consumable items. The basic idea here is to deliver, on a regular basis, stocks of this product to your customers until they ask you not to. But get their agreement first—and their credit card or other charge details.
- **Plan future purchases.** If you sell a product that is regularly updated, offer to assist your customers by planning their future purchases for them. Let them know when the new model or product is about to be released and make arrangements for it to be delivered. You could offer to automatically trade in their old, outdated model, even at a prearranged price.

- **Offer on the next purchase.** These deals amount to giving the customer a gift check or discount voucher to spend when they make their next purchase. They work particularly well in restaurants.
- **Reminder system.** This works wonderfully for mechanical workshops, dentists, hairdressers, or any other business where people return regularly by taking care of the things customers tend to forget. Sending a reminder to someone is also a great reason for staying in touch.
- **Increase credit levels.** If your customers are good payers, why not offer to increase their credit levels as a reward? But be sure they can meet their payment deadlines.
- **Target likely repeaters.** This is a great way to build a business based on repeat business. And it's simple—chase the right customers in the first place. Who buys from you on a regular basis? Find out and offer them a great incentive to keep coming back. Try to identify their buying patterns and focus your attentions on appealing to them.
- **Postpurchase reassurance.** Make your customers feel great about their purchasing decisions. Why not mail them press articles about the product they've just bought? It's another great reason for keeping in touch. How about mailing them testimonials from your other customers? Or send them a thank-you card.
- **Suggest alternative uses.** Mail your customers an information sheet detailing different ways the product they've bought can be used. Not only will it add to their satisfaction, it'll provide you with yet another reason for keeping in touch.

Management-Related Strategies

There are certain management decisions that can have a dramatic effect on your number of transactions. Now they may not apply to some types of business, and they may not be suitable in all situations, but they are certainly worth considering. They include:

- Offer *big* customers a shareholding in your business. Imagine that! But why not? I mean, if a customer gives you the majority of his business, it makes good business sense doing everything you can to retain his business.

Forever. Once a customer has a stake in your business, he'll do everything possible to ensure that your business does well, won't he? He'll tell all his friends and acquaintances about your business. But if you do decide to go down this route, seek professional advice first. An accountant will tell you how it's best done.

- Sell more consumables. If you sell a product that makes use of consumables, you're missing out on a potentially lucrative market. Why let another company benefit from your customer? But do be aware that the consumables market is often highly price-competitive. Hefty discounting is the order of the day. You'll need to give your customers good reason to switch their buying patterns to deal with you in this regard. But many prefer to deal with a one-stop shop.

Train your team. Run regular training sessions in which team members can share their recent experiences and ways of satisfying customers. Encourage them to provide feedback. If something worked with one team member, you'd want the others to emulate it, as it's likely to work again. This strategy is not only good for helping to increase your number of transactions; it's also great for team morale.

Testing and Measuring

It was now time to talk Charlie through everything he needed to know about testing and measuring. He had progressed famously from the time he first asked me to discuss his business with him. He kept an open mind throughout and was prepared to listen to what I had to say.

Then he implemented what I suggested, and he saw immediate results.

"You'll have noticed I've been stressing the importance of testing and measuring from the time I first began coaching you, Charlie," I said.

"Every topic we've discussed, no matter what part of the Business Chassis it belonged to, has been underpinned by testing and measuring. So now it's time to look at this area in more detail."

"Great, Brad. As you know, when dealing with cars, this forms the basis of what we do as well. So I'm right with you. You're talking my language."

"As usual, I'm going to revert to basics to get going. But remember, just because we're discussing testing and measuring today, that doesn't mean it relates only to generating repeat business; use this information for generating leads, promoting your business, and closing sales as well."

Why Test and Measure?

If you don't know where your customers come from, you're really stabbing around in the dark. You'll have no real idea which marketing campaigns are working, how well your salespeople are doing, or even how much each sale is costing you.

Once you know these things, you have the power to make decisions, and good ones at that. You'll know which marketing campaigns to kill, which to improve, and which to spend more money on.

You'll also know where your key leverage point is—that is, the thing that you most need to improve. Perhaps your conversion rate is high but your leads are few—maybe it's the other way around. Maybe you're doing well in both lead generation and conversion, but you're not selling enough high-priced items.

Once you know which area needs work, you can start to make some new, well-informed marketing decisions.

At the end of this section I've included testing and measuring sheets designed for specific types of businesses. Pick the one that suits you best, but if yours is a specific situation, feel free to make the necessary changes.

The Three Most Important Things about Testing and Measuring

1. Testing and measuring is nothing new. You've probably been doing it all your business life. Remember the newspaper advertising you tried that didn't work, and the radio spots that did? That's all testing is. It's about finding out what produces results and what doesn't, then making decisions based on that.

2. You *must* start asking people where they found out about you. If you don't, you'll be operating in the dark forever. You may keep running an ad that never brings in a sale, or you may accidentally kill a good one. Customers usually come from so many sources it's impossible to judge how an ad is working on sales alone. Perhaps you got more referrals that week, or there may have been a festival in town. Every time someone buys, ask them this question: "By the way, can I just ask where you heard about my business?" No one, and I mean no one, will have any problem telling you.

3. Be vigilant and disciplined. You can't test and measure half the time; you must do it every hour of every day. It's not difficult—just remember to mark down a record after every customer interaction. And make sure your employees do the same. Stress the importance of it and absolutely *demand* that they do. Also, tell them it's essential that they are honest.

What to Do with Your Results

The first thing to do is to see what's not working. If an ad is getting a very low response (which means the profit margin from the sales is not at least paying for the ad), kill it.

Of course, you need to consider the lifetime value of the customer as well. If, after taking all factors taken into account, you're not getting results, bite the bullet and stop running it. Every time you run this sort of ad, you're literally giving away money.

Now you have two options—channel your marketing funds elsewhere (like back into your pocket) or improve the ad.

If you choose option two, there are a couple of things you can do to make the task simpler. First, go back over your past ads and think about how well each one worked. Pull out the best couple and see if you can pick what gave them their edge. Next, read a couple of books on marketing, or at least flip through them. Then look at what your competitors are doing. Do they have an ad that they run every week? Unless they're stupid, this ad must be doing OK. What ideas can you borrow from it?

Then write a new ad. Don't do anything with it yet—we'll get to that in a minute.

Go through this process with each marketing piece that doesn't seem to be working. By this I mean examine your letters, Yellow Pages, referral systems, flyers and so on.

Kill, examine, modify. Kill, examine, modify. Once you have a collection of revised pieces, just sit on them—there's something more important we need to deal with first, and that's the strategies that are working.

Run through each of the working strategies in depth, examining why they are producing results and the others aren't. See if you can pick the one important, attractive point about each. This in itself will teach you a great deal about your business.

Next, think of a way to do each strategy on a larger scale. If it's flyers you're looking at, the answer is simple—deliver twice as many. That should bring twice the sales. If it's an ad, run it in more papers, or increase its size. If it's Yellow Pages, book a bigger space next time.

But whatever you do, don't meddle—just do the same thing on a larger scale.

After that, test and measure for another two weeks. Notice if the number of enquiries remains the same or goes down. Also compare this with how much you're spending on marketing.

You'll probably find you barely miss those dud strategies and the "larger scale" working strategies are paying off nicely. If it's not, return to the original size.

Conversion is the number of enquiries that become sales. You may find you get one in 10, 99 out of a 100, or anything in between.

Leave it for a month or so and work on converting the leads you have. A better conversion technique, plus more leads from bigger-scale successful marketing strategies should give your business a boost.

The lack of dead money being poured into ads that don't work should also give you a helping hand.

After running through this process, it's time to pull your revised "dud" strategies out of the drawer, and give them a run.

Do one at a time, and track the result meticulously. Note exactly how many leads it brings you, and how many of those turn into sales. Compare that with the marketing cost, and judge whether the strategy has been good.

If so, add it to your list of ongoing strategies. If not, don't give up hope. Try it again, testing a different headline, medium, offer, look, etc. Change a meaningful part and measure the results. If it doesn't work again, give it one more try. If you get the feeling that *nothing* is going to work, abandon the idea, as it's probably the wrong approach altogether and concentrate your efforts somewhere else.

Very soon, you'll develop a collection of marketing strategies that work. Now that's a business success formula, and the real benefit of testing and measuring.

How to Use the Retail Daily Testing and Measuring Sheet

This sheet is ideal for all types of retail stores, especially those with mid- to high-priced items. Give each member of your team a testing and measuring sheet. Total all sheets up at the end of the day, and then do a weekly total. Add these up to form your monthly total. Once you've done this, examine the sheets to work out which strategies have been working.

Prospect's Name: The name of the customer. You need to ask them for it. If you don't get a chance to get their name, simply write a basic description of them, such as "Male 30s" or "Female 50s."

Repeat Customer (New Inquiry): Tick this column if the customer is an old one, yet they have come in to discuss a new purchase. By this I mean one they haven't previously talked to you about. It may be a product they've bought before—just as long as this is the first time you've talked to them about buying it this time around.

Repeat Customer (Same Inquiry): Tick this column if the customer is an old customer and you have discussed the product or service before. That means you have talked to him about the specific purchase he is considering making.

New Customers (How Did They Hear about You?): Fill this out if the customer is entirely new. That is, she has never been in before. Ask her where she heard about you. Don't suggest anything if she takes a while to answer—wait for her response.

New Customers (Which Marketing Strategy?): This applies when you are testing different versions of the one type of marketing strategy. For example, you may be running three different ads over a three-week period. Give each one a code, and fill it in here.

Details Captured: Tick this column if you get the person's full name, address, and phone number. Just say, "I'd like to put you on our mailing list. Could I get your details, please?"

Sales Conversion (Sale Made): Tick this if a sale is made.

Sales Conversion (Sale Value): Write in the value of the sale.

Sales Conversion (Follow Up/Call Back): Tick this column if the customer does not buy and is to be followed up later. Alternately, tick this if the customer claims they will come back.

Average Dollar Sale: Divide the total takings for the day by the number of sales for the day. This will give you your average dollar sale.

Conversion Rate Percent: Divide the total number of customers by the number that actually made a purchase. This will give you your conversion rate.

How to Use the Service Daily Testing and Measuring Sheet

This sheet is ideal for all types of service businesses, especially those that don't quote.

Each testing and measuring sheet is for an individual member of the team. Total all sheets up at the end of the day, then do a weekly total. Add these up to form your monthly total. Once you've done this, examine the sheets to work out which strategies have been working.

Prospect's Name: The name of the customer. You need to ask him for it. If you don't get a chance to get his name, simply write a basic description of him, such as "Male 30s" or "Female 50s."

Repeat Customer (New Inquiry): Tick this column if the customer is an old one, yet she hasn't come in to discuss a new purchase. That is, one she hasn't previously talked to you about. It may be a service she's bought before—just as long as this is the first time you've talked to her about buying it this time around.

Repeat Customer (Same Inquiry): Tick this column if the customer is an old customer, and you have discussed the service before. By this I mean you have talked to her about the specific purchase they are considering.

New Customers (How Did They Hear about You?): Fill this out if the customer is entirely new. That is, he has never been in before. Ask him where he heard about you. Don't suggest anything if he takes a while to answer—wait for his response.

New Customers (Which Marketing Strategy?): This applies when you are testing different versions of the one type of marketing strategy. For example, you may be running three different ads over a 3-week period. Give each one a code, and fill it in here.

Details Captured: Tick this column if you get the person's full name, address, and phone number. Just say, "I'd like to put you on our mailing list. Could I get your details, please?"

Sales Conversion (Appointment/Sale Made): Tick this if an appointment or sale is made.

Sales Conversion (Sale Value): Write in the value of the sale.

Sales Conversion (Follow Up/Call Back): Tick this column if the customer does not make an appointment and is to be followed up later. Alternately, tick the column if the customer claims he will come back.

Average Dollar Sale: Divide the total takings for the day by the number of sales for the day. This will give you your average dollar sale.

Conversion Rate Percent: Divide the total number of customers by the number that actually made a purchase. This will give you your conversion rate.

How to Use the Wholesale Testing and Measuring Sheet

This sheet is ideal for all types of wholesale businesses, especially those that don't quote. Each testing and measuring sheet is for an individual member of the team. Total all sheets up at the end of the day, then do a weekly total. Add these up to form your monthly total. Once you've done this, examine the sheets to work out which strategies have been working.

Prospect's Name: The name of the customer/business. You need to ask her for it.

Repeat Customer (New Inquiry): Tick this column if the customer is an old one, yet they have come in to discuss a new purchase—that is, one he hasn't previously talked to you about. It may be a product he has bought before, just as long as this is the first time you've talked to him about buying it this time around.

Repeat Customer (Same Inquiry): Tick this column if the customer is an old customer and you have discussed the product before. This means you have talked to her about the specific purchase she is considering.

New Customers (How Did They Hear about You?): Fill this out if the customer is entirely new. He has never been in before. Ask him where he heard about you. Don't suggest anything if he takes a while to answer—wait for his response.

New Customers (Which Marketing Strategy?): This applies when you are testing different versions of the one type of marketing strategy. For example, you may be running three different ads over a three-week period. Give each one a code, and fill it in here.

Details Captured: Tick this column if you get the person's full name, address, and phone number. Just say, "I'd like to put you on our mailing list. Could I get your details, please?"

Sales Conversion (Order Taken): Tick this if an order is taken.

Sales Conversion (Order Value): Write in the value of the order.

Sales Conversion (Follow Up/Call Back): Tick this column if the customer does not make an order and is to be followed up later. Alternately, tick the column if the customer claims they will come back.

Average Dollar Sale: Divide the total takings for the day by the number of sales for the day. This will give you your average dollar sale.

Conversion Rate Percent: Divide the total number of customers by the number that actually made a purchase. This will give you your conversion rate.

How to Use the Daily Service Testing and Measuring Sheet

This sheet is ideal for all types of service businesses, especially those with a long sales process and a quoting system. Each testing and measuring sheet is for an individual member of the team. Total all sheets up at the end of the day, then do a weekly total. Add these up to form your monthly total. Once you've done this, examine the sheets to work out which strategies have been working.

Prospect's Name: The name of the customer. You need to ask him for it. If you don't get a chance to get his name, simply write a basic description of him, like "Male 30s" or "Female 50s."

Repeat Customer (New Inquiry): Tick this column if the customer is an old one, yet she has come in to discuss a new purchase—that is, one she hasn't previously talked to you about. It may be a service she's bought before—just as long as this is the first time you've talked to her about buying it this time around.

Repeat Customer (Same Inquiry): Tick this column if the customer is an old customer, and you have discussed the service before. That means you have talked to him about the specific purchase he is considering.

New Customers (How Did They Hear about You?): Fill this out if the customer is entirely new—that is, she has never been in before. Ask her where she heard about you. Don't suggest anything if she takes a while to answer—wait for her response.

New Customers (Which Marketing Strategy?): This applies when you are testing different versions of the one type of marketing strategy. For example, you may be running three different ads over a three-week period. Give each one a code, and fill it in here.

Details Captured: Tick this column if you get the person's full name, address, and phone number. Just say, "I'd like to put you on our mailing list. Could I get your details, please?"

Sales Conversion (Quote Requested): Tick this if a quote is asked for.

Sales Conversion (Sale Value): If you make a sale, write in the value of the sale.

Sales Conversion (Follow Up/Call Back): Tick this column if the customer does not ask for a quote or buy and is to be followed up later. Alternately, tick the column if the customer claims he will come back.

Average Dollar Sale: Divide the total takings for the day by the number of sales for the day. This will give you your average dollar sale.

Conversion Rate Percent: Divide the total number of customers by the number that actually made a purchase. This will give you your conversion rate. Do not include the customers who have asked for a quote in your 'number of customers'.

How to Use the Busy Retail Daily Testing and Measuring Sheet

This sheet is ideal for busy retail stores and fast food outlets, especially those with low-priced, high-turnover items. Each testing and measuring sheet is for an individual member of the team. Total all sheets up at the end of the day, then do a weekly total. Add these up to form your monthly total. Once you've done this, examine the sheets to work out which strategies have been working.

Walk-In Tally: Simply make a mark in this column each time a customer walks in. You may want to note down the customer's sex and a rough idea of the customer's age. This will help you work out your target market.

Repeat Customer: Tick this column if the customer has bought from you before.

New Customers (How Did They Hear about You?): Fill this out if the customer is entirely new—that is, he has never been in before. Ask him where he heard about you. Don't suggest anything if he takes a while to answer—wait for his response.

New Customers (Which Marketing Strategy?): This applies when you are testing different versions of the one type of marketing strategy. For example, you may be running three different ads over a 3-week period. Give each one a code, and fill it in here.

Details Captured: Tick this column if you get the person's full name, address, and phone number. Just say, "I'd like to put you on our mailing list. Could I get your details, please?"

Sales Conversion (Sale Value): Fill in the value of any sale made.

Sales Conversion (Follow Up/Call Back): Tick this column if the customer claims she will come back.

Average Dollar Sale: Divide the total takings for the day by the number of sales for the day. This will give you your average dollar sale.

Conversion Rate Percent: Divide the total number of customers by the number that actually made a purchase. This will give you your conversion rate.

How to Use the Restaurant Daily Testing and Measuring Sheet

This sheet is ideal for restaurants and other similar businesses. Each testing and measuring sheet is for an individual member of the team. Total all sheets up at the end of the day, then do a weekly total. Add these up to form your monthly total. Once you've done this, examine the sheets to work out which strategies have been working.

Prospect's Name: Find out the name of the prospect and write it here.

Repeat Customer: Tick this column if the customer has bought from you before.

New Customers (How Did They Hear about You?): Fill this out if the customer is entirely new—that is, she has never been in before. Ask her where she heard about you. Don't suggest anything if she takes a while to answer—wait for her response.

New Customers (Which Marketing Strategy?): This applies when you are testing different versions of the one type of marketing strategy. For example, you may be running three different ads over a three-week period. Give each one a code, and fill it in here.

Details Captured: Tick this column if you get the person's full name, address, and phone number. Just say, "I'd like to put you on our mailing list. Could I get your details, please?"

Sales Conversion (Booking Taken): Tick if a booking is taken.

Sales Conversion (Sale Value): Fill in the value of any sale made.

Sales Conversion (Follow Up/Call Back): Tick this column if the customer claims he will come back.

Average Dollar Sale: Divide the total takings for the day by the number of sales for the day. This will give you your average dollar sale.

Conversion Rate Percent: Divide the total number of customers by the number that actually made a purchase. This will give you your conversion rate.

How to Use the Direct Mail Daily Testing and Measuring Sheet

This sheet is ideal for direct mail campaigns, regardless of the business. Each testing and measuring sheet is for an individual member of the team. Total all sheets up at the end of the day, then do a weekly total. Add these up to form your monthly total. Once you've done this, examine the sheets to work out which strategies have been working.

Prospect's Name: Find out the name of the prospect and write it here.

Marketing Strategy/Piece/Offer: Write down the code of the direct mail piece you are sending to the person. This is very useful if you are testing numerous direct mail letters.

Phoned (Contacted): Tick this column if you actually make contact with the person when phoning.

Phone (Unavailable: Need To Phone Back): Tick this column if you are unable to get in contact with the person.

Received Letter: Tick this column if the prospect says she received the letter.

Sales Conversion (Appointment/Sale Made): Tick this column if a sale is made or an appointment time is booked.

Sales Conversion (Sale Value): Fill in the value of any sale made.

Sales Conversion (Follow Up/Call Back): Tick this column if you need to follow the customer up again, or he claims he will come back.

Average Dollar Sale: Divide the total takings for the day by the number of sales for the day. This will give you your average dollar sale.

Conversion Rate Percent: Divide the total number of customers by the number that actually made a purchase. This will give you your conversion rate.

How to Use the Networking Daily Testing and Measuring Sheet

This sheet is ideal for network marketers and other similar businesses. Each testing and measuring sheet is for an individual. Total all sheets up at the end of the day, then do a weekly total. Add these up to form your monthly total. Once you've done this, examine the sheets to work out which strategies have been working.

Prospect's Name: Find out the name of the prospect and write it here.

Follow-Up Prospect: Tick this column if you have presented to the customer before.

New Customers (They Initiated Contact): Fill this out if the customer is entirely new. Tick it if the prospect initiated contact with you.

New Customers (You Initiated Contact): Fill this out if the customer is entirely new. Tick it if you initiated contact with the prospect.

Comments on Presentation: Write any meaningful comments on your presentation. "Went well," "Not interested," "With another company," or something else.

Sales Conversion (Sale/Recruitment Made): Tick if the person buys something or decides to become a part of your network or downline.

Sales Conversion (Follow Up/Call Back): Tick this column if you need to follow up the customer again.

Conversion Rate Percent: Divide the total number of customers by the number that actually made a purchase. This will give you your conversion rate.

How to Use the Telemarketing Daily Testing and Measuring Sheet

This sheet is ideal for all types of telemarketing-based businesses. Each testing and measuring sheet is for an individual member of the team. Total all sheets up at the end of the day, then do a weekly total. Add these up to form your monthly total. Once you've done this, examine the sheets to work out which strategies have been working.

Prospect's Name: The name of the customer. You should have it on your list.

New Prospect (List): Write down which list the name appears on. It may be your past customer list, a bought list, or another one entirely.

New Prospect (Offer Script): Write down which offer or script you are using. You may want to use codes to identify each one.

Follow-Up Prospect: Tick this column if you have phoned the prospect before.

Sales Conversion (Sale Made): Tick this if a sale is made.

Sales Conversion (Sale Value): Write in the value of the sale.

Sales Conversion (Follow Up/Call Back): Tick this column if the customer is to be followed up later. Alternately, tick the column if the customer claims she will call back.

Average Dollar Sale: Divide the total takings for the day by the number of sales for the day. This will give you your average dollar sale.

Conversion Rate Percent: Divide the total number of customers by the number that actually made a purchase. This will give you your conversion rate.

How to Use the Professional Daily Testing and Measuring Sheet

This sheet is ideal for all types of professional business (doctors, solicitors, etc.). Each testing and measuring sheet is for an individual member of the team. Total all sheets up at the end of the day, then do a weekly total. Add these up to form your monthly total. Once you've done this, examine the sheets to work out which strategies have been working.

Prospect's Name: The name of the customer. You need to ask him for it. If you don't get a chance to get his name, simply write a basic description of him, like "Male 30s" or "Female 50s."

Repeat Customer (New Inquiry): Tick this column if the customer is an old one, yet she has come in to discuss a new service—that is, one she hasn't previously talked to you about. It may be a service she's bought before—just as long as this is the first time you've talked to her about buying it this time around.

Repeat Customer (Same Inquiry): Tick this column if the customer is an old customer and you have discussed the service before. That means you have talked to him about the specific service he is considering.

New Customers (How Did They Hear about You?): Fill this out if the customer is entirely new—that is, she has never been in before. Ask her where she heard about you. Don't suggest anything if she takes a while to answer—wait for her response.

New Customers (Which Marketing Strategy?): This applies when you are testing different versions of the one type of marketing strategy. For example, you may be running three different ads over a three-week period. Give each one a code, and fill it in here.

Sales Conversion (Appointment Made): Tick here if an appointment is made.

Sales Conversion (Appointment Dollar Value): The value of the appointment or the sale.

Sales Conversion (Details Captured): Tick this column if you get the full details of the customer.

Sales Conversion (Booked Again): Tick this column if the customer books in his next appointment now.

Sales Conversion (Follow Up/Call Back): Tick this column if the customer is to be followed up later. Alternately, tick the column if the customer claims he will come back.

Average Dollar Sale: Divide the total takings for the day by the number of sales for the day. This will give you your average dollar sale.

Conversion Rate Percent: Divide the total number of customers by the number that actually made a purchase. This will give you your conversion rate.

How to Use the Party Plan Daily Testing and Measuring Sheet

This sheet is ideal for businesses that sell products via party plans, and other similar businesses. Each testing and measuring sheet is for an individual member of the team. Total all sheets up at the end of the day, then do a weekly total. Add these up to form your monthly total. Once you've done this, examine the sheets to work out which strategies have been working.

Attendee's Name: Find out the name of the prospect and write it here.

New Attendee (How Did They Hear about You?): Fill this out if the customer is entirely new—that is, she's never been to one of your presentations before. Ask her where she heard about you. Don't suggest anything if she takes a while to answer—wait for her response.

New Attendee (Which Marketing Strategy?): This applies when you are testing different versions of the one type of marketing strategy. For example, you may be running three different ads over a three-week period. Give each one a code and fill it in here.

Repeat Attendee: Tick this column if the customer has bought from you before.

Sales Conversion (Sale Made): Tick if a sale is made.

Sales Conversion (Sale $$ Value): Fill in the value of any sale made.

Sales Conversion (Follow Up/Invite Again): Tick this column if the person is to be invited to another party or followed up.

Average Dollar Sale: Divide the total takings for the day by the number of sales for the day. This will give you your average dollar sale.

Conversion Rate Percent: Divide the total number of customers by the number that actually made a purchase. This will give you your conversion rate.

Retail Daily Testing & Measuring Sheet

Name: ____________________ **Date:** ______________

Inquiry #	Prospects Name	Repeat Customer		New Customer		Details Captured Y / N	Sales Conversion		
		New Enquiry	Same Enquiry	How Did They Hear About You	Which Marketing Strategy		Sale Made	Sale Value	Follow Up/Call Back
1									
2									
3									
4									
5									
6									
7									
8									
9									
10									
11									
12									
13									
TOTALS									

AVG $$ SALE = (Total of Sales Value column / Total No. of Sales Made) ________ / ________ = ________

CONVERSION RATE % = (Total No of Customers / Total No. of Sales Made) ________ / ________ = ________

Service Daily Testing & Measuring Sheet

Name: ____________________ **Date:** ______________

Inquiry #	Prospects Name	Repeat Customer		New Customer		Details Captured Y / N	Sales Conversion		
		New Enquiry	Same Enquiry	How Did They Hear About You	Which Marketing Strategy		Appt / Sale Made	Sale Value	Follow Up/Call Back
1									
2									
3									
4									
5									
6									
7									
8									
9									
10									
11									
12									
13									
TOTALS									

AVG $$ SALE = (Total of Sales Value column / Total No. of Sales Made) ________ / ________ = ________

CONVERSION RATE % = (Total No of Customers / Total No. of Sales Made) ________ / ________ = ________

Wholesale Testing & Measuring Sheet

Name: ____________________ **Date:** ______________

Inquiry #	Prospects Name	Repeat Customer		New Customer		Details Captured Y / N	Sales Conversion		
		New Enquiry	Same Enquiry	How Did They Hear About You	Which Marketing Strategy		Order Taken	Order Value	Follow Up/Call Back
1									
2									
3									
4									
5									
6									
7									
8									
9									
10									
11									
12									
13									
TOTALS									

AVG $$ SALE = (Total of Sales Value column / Total No. of Sales Made) ________ / ________ = ________

CONVERSION RATE % = (Total No of Customers / Total No. of Sales Made) ________ / ________ = ________

Daily Service Testing & Measuring Sheet

Name: ____________________ **Date:** ______________

Inquiry #	Prospects Name	Repeat Customer		New Customer		Details Captured Y / N	Sales Conversion		
		New Enquiry	Same Enquiry	How Did They Hear About You	Which Marketing Strategy		Quote Requested	Sale Value	Follow Up/Call Back
1									
2									
3									
4									
5									
6									
7									
8									
9									
10									
11									
12									
13									
TOTALS									

AVG $$ SALE = (Total of Sales Value column / Total No. of Sales Made) ________ / ________ = ________

CONVERSION RATE % = (Total No of Customers / Total No. of Sales Made) ________ / ________ = ________

Busy Retail Daily Testing & Measuring Sheet

Name: ____________________ **Date:** ______________

Inquiry #	Walk-In Tally	Repeat Customer	New Customer		Details Captured Y / N	Sales Conversion		
			How Did They Hear About You	Which Marketing Strategy		Sale Made	Sale Value	Follow Up/Call Back
1								
2								
3								
4								
5								
6								
7								
8								
9								
10								
11								
12								
13								
TOTALS								

AVG $$ SALE = (Total of Sales Value column / Total No. of Sales Made) __________ / __________ = __________

CONVERSION RATE % = (Total No of Customers / Total No. of Sales Made) __________ / __________ = __________

Restaurant Daily Testing & Measuring Sheet

Name: ____________________ **Date:** ______________

Inquiry #	Prospects Name	Repeat Customer	New Customer		Details Captured Y / N	Sales Conversion		
			How Did They Hear About You	Which Marketing Strategy		Booking Taken	Sale Value	Follow Up/Call Back
1								
2								
3								
4								
5								
6								
7								
8								
9								
10								
11								
12								
13								
TOTALS								

AVG $$ SALE = (Total of Sales Value column / Total No. of Sales Made) __________ / __________ = __________

CONVERSION RATE % = (Total No of Customers / Total No. of Sales Made) __________ / __________ = __________

Direct Mail Daily Testing & Measuring Sheet

Name: ________________ Date: ____________

Inquiry #	Prospects Name	Marketing Strategy/Piece /Offer	Telephoned		Received Letter Y / N	Sales Conversion		
			Contacted	Unavailable: Need to call back		Appt/ Sale Made	Sale Value	Follow Up/Call Back
1								
2								
3								
4								
5								
6								
7								
8								
9								
10								
11								
12								
13								
TOTALS								

AVG $$ SALE = (Total of Sales Value column / Total No. of Sales Made) ________ / ________ = ________

CONVERSION RATE % = (Total No of Customers / Total No. of Sales Made) ________ / ________ = ________

Networking Daily Testing & Measuring Sheet

Name: ________________ Date: ____________

Inquiry #	Prospects Name	Follow Up Prospect	New Customer		Comments on Present-ation	Sales Conversion		
			They Initiated Contact	You Initiated Contact		Sale/ Recruitment Made	Sale Value	Follow Up/Call Back
1								
2								
3								
4								
5								
6								
7								
8								
9								
10								
11								
12								
13								
TOTALS								

AVG $$ SALE = (Total of Sales Value column / Total No. of Sales Made) ________ / ________ = ________

CONVERSION RATE % = (Total No of Customers / Total No. of Sales Made) ________ / ________ = ________

Telemarketing Daily Testing & Measuring Sheet

Name: ____________________ **Date:** ________________

Inquiry #	Prospects Name	New Prospect		Follow Up Prospect	Details Captured Y / N	Sales Conversion		
		List	Offer Script			Sale Made	Sale Value	Follow Up/Call Back
1								
2								
3								
4								
5								
6								
7								
8								
9								
10								
11								
12								
13								
TOTALS								

AVG $$ SALE = (Total of Sales Value column / Total No. of Sales Made) ________ / ________ = ________

CONVERSION RATE % = (Total No of Customers / Total No. of Sales Made) ________ / ________ = ________

Professional Daily Testing & Measuring Sheet

Name: ________________ **Date:** ________________

Inquiry #	Prospects Name	Repeat Customer		New Customer		Appt Made Y / N	Sales Conversion			Follow Up/Call Back
		New Enquiry	Same Enquiry	How Did They Hear About You	Which Marketing Strategy		Appt $$ Value	Details Captured	Booked Again	
1										
2										
3										
4										
5										
6										
7										
8										
9										
10										
11										
12										
13										
TOTALS										

AVG $$ SALE = (Total of Sales Value column / Total No. of Sales Made) ________ / ________ = ________

CONVERSION RATE % = (Total No of Customers / Total No. of Sales Made) ________ / ________ = ________

Party Plan Daily Testing & Measuring Sheet

Name: ______________ **Date:** ______________

Inquiry #	Attendees Name	Repeat Attendee	New Attendee		Details Captured Y / N	Sales Conversion		
			How Did They Hear About You	Which Marketing Strategy		Sale Made	Sale $$ Value	Follow Up/Invite Again
1								
2								
3								
4								
5								
6								
7								
8								
9								
10								
11								
12								
13								
TOTALS								

AVG $$ SALE = (Total of Sales Value column / Total No. of Sales Made) ________ / ________ = ________

CONVERSION RATE % = (Total No of Customers / Total No. of Sales Made) ________ / ________ = ________

Break-Even Analysis

"Charlie, another vital factor to take into account is your break-even analysis. You need to know exactly what each strategy is costing you."

"Yes, I can understand that, Brad. It has crossed my mind that some of the strategies we've discussed may not work well enough to cover the cost of implementing them."

"And by the same token, some might work really well. The point is it's essential you work out your costs up front. Otherwise, you'll have no idea what you need to achieve in order for the campaign to be worthwhile."

I explained that it might turn out that after doing the analysis, he could discover the campaign has so little chance of success, he'd need to go back to the drawing board altogether.

This analysis is for the whole campaign. After working out the total fixed costs (for the campaign), the level of profit needs to be worked out (the average dollar sale minus variable costs), which should provide enough information to work out how many responses are needed in order to break even.

"Divide this number by the total number of marketing pieces you are planning to send out. This will give you a percentage response rate. As a very rough guide (every case is different), anything over 15 percent is stretching it. If you need that high a response, you might night to have another think about it."

The very best campaigns get a response rate of around 15 percent. The best direct mail campaigns to existing clients can achieve around 60 percent. These are rare results. If you need higher than that to break even, reassess whether direct mail is the best way to go.

Now, fill in the blanks in the form provided here to work out your required response rate.

Hard Costs

Advertising	$ ....
Envelopes	$ ....
Paper	$ ....
Printing	$ ....

Postage	$ ....
Other	$ ....
1. Total Fixed Costs	**$ ....**
2. Average Dollar Sale	**$ ....**
Variable Costs	
Telephone	$ ....
Wages	$ ....
Electricity	$ ....
Rent	$ ....
Brochures	$ ....
Other Postage	$ ....
Other	$ ....
3. Total Variables	**$ ....**
Delivery Costs	
Cost Of Goods Sold	$ ....
Taxes	$ ....
Transportation	$ ....
Packaging	$ ....
Other	$ ....
4. Total Delivery	**$ ....**
5. Net Profit [2/(3+4)]	**$ ....**
6. Response Needed to Break Even (1/5)	**$ ....**

Conclusion

So there you have it—everything you need to improve your number of transactions.

Repeat business strategies serve a very important purpose in business—any business. First, they focus your mind and attention on what needs to be done to maximize your chances of achieving your business goals by generating more repeat business. Second, by developing them you could learn things about your business you never knew before.

Once you've worked your way through this book, you'll know how to produce effective newsletters. You'll know what it takes to hold successful closed-door sales and how to develop fantastically loyal customers that will be the envy of all your competitors. You'll also know how to come up with great offers that will keep your customers waiting in anticipation for the next one.

But that's not all. You will know how to focus your stock, sales, and management-related strategies on reinforcing efforts already in place to bolster repeat purchase business. And you'll know more about providing sensational customer service than anyone else in your neighborhood.

By the time you've worked your way though this book, you'll also know the true value of testing and measuring. You'll have seen the value of incorporating it into your daily routine. And you'll also be able to accurately analyze the costs of implementing the various strategies chosen.

So what are you waiting for? It's time to get into *Action.*

Getting into *Action*

So, when is the best time to start?

Now—right now—so let me give you a step-by-step method to get yourself onto the same success path of many of my clients and the clients of my team at *Action International.*

Start testing and measuring now.

You'll want to ask your customers and prospects how they found out about you and your business. This will give you an idea of what's been working and what hasn't. You also want to concentrate on the five areas of the business chassis. Remember:

1. Number of Leads from each campaign.
2. Conversion Rate from each and every campaign.
3. Number of Transactions on average per year per customer.
4. Average Dollar Sale from each campaign.
5. Your Margins on each product or service.

The Number of Leads is easy; just take a measure for four weeks, average it out, and multiply by 50 working weeks of the year. Of course you'd ask each lead where they came from so you've got enough information to make advertising decisions.

The Conversion Rate is a little trickier, not because it's hard to measure, but because we want to know a few more details. You want to know what level of conversion you have from each and every type of marketing strategy you use. Remember that some customers won't buy right away, so keep accurate records on each and every lead.

To find the Number of Transactions you'll need to go through your records. Hopefully you can find the transaction history of at least 50 of your past customers and then average out their yearly purchases.

The Average Dollar Sale is as simple as it sounds. The total dollars sold divided by the number of sales. The best information you can collect is the average from each marketing campaign you run, so that you know where the real profit is coming from.

And, of course, your margins. An Average Margin is good to know and measure, but to know the margins on everything you sell is the most powerful knowledge you can collect.

If you're having any challenges with your testing and measuring, be sure to contact your nearest *Action International* Business Coach. She'll be able to help you through and show you the specialized documents to use.

If, by chance, you're thinking of racing ahead before you test and measure, remember this. It's impossible to improve a score when you don't know what the score is.

So you've got your starting point. You know exactly what's going on in your business right now. In fact, you know more about not only what's happening right now, but also the factors that are going to create what will happen tomorrow.

The next step in your business growth is simple.

Let's decide what you want out of the business—in other words, your goals. Here are the main points I want you to plan for.

How many hours do you want to work each week? How much money do you want to take out of the business each month? And, most importantly, when do you want to finish the business?

By "finish" the business, I mean when it will be systematized enough so it can run without your having to be there. Remember this about business; a little bit of planning goes a long way, but to make a plan you have to have a destination.

Once again, if you're having difficulty, talk to an *Action International* Business Coach. He'll know exactly how to help you find what it is you really want out of both your business and your life.

Now the real work begins.

Remember, our goal is to get a 10 percent increase in each area over the next 12 months. Choose well, but I want to warn you of one thing, one thing I can literally guarantee.

Eight out of 10 marketing campaigns you run *will not work.*

That's why when you choose to run, say, an advertising campaign in your local newspaper, you've got to run at least 10 different ads. When you select a direct mail campaign, you should send out at least 10 different letters to test, and so on.

Make sure you get at least five strategies under each heading and plan to run at least one, preferably two, at least each month for the next 12 months.

Don't work on just one of the five areas at a time; mix it up a little so you get the synergy of all five areas working together.

Now, this is the most important advice I can give you:

Learn how to make each and every strategy work. Don't just think you know what to do; go through my hints and tips, read more books, listen to as many tapes as you can, watch all the videos you can find, talk to the experts, and make sure you get the most advantage you can before you invest a whole lot of money.

The next 12 months are going to be a matter of doing the numbers, running the campaigns, testing headlines, testing offers, testing prices, and, of course, measuring the results.

By the end of it you should have at least five new strategies in each of the five areas working together to produce a great result.

Once again I want to stress that this will work and this will make your business grow as long as *you* work it.

Is it simple? *Yes.*

Is it easy? *No.*

You'll have to work hard. If you can get the guidance of someone who's been there before you, then get it.

Whatever you do, start it now, start it today, and most importantly, make the most of every day. Your past does not equal your future; you decide your future right here and right now.

Be who you want to be, *do* what you need to do, in order to *have* what you want to have.

Positive *thought* without positive *Action* leaves you with positively *nothing.* I called my company *Action International,* not Theory International, or Yeah, I read that book International, but *Action International.*

So take the first step—and get into *Action.*

ABOUT THE AUTHOR

Bradley J. Sugars

Brad Sugars is a world-renowned Australian entrepreneur, author, and business coach who has helped more than a million clients around the world find business and personal success.

He's a trained accountant, but as he puts it, most of his experience comes from owning his own companies. Brad's been in business for himself since age 15 in some way or another, although his father would argue he started at 7 when he was caught selling his Christmas presents to his brothers. He's owned and operated more than two dozen companies, from pizza to ladies fashion, from real estate to insurance and many more.

His main company, *Action International*, started from humble beginnings in the back bedroom of a suburban home in 1993 when Brad started teaching business owners how to grow their sales and marketing results. Now *Action* has nearly 1000 franchises in 19 countries and is ranked in the top 100 franchises in the world.

Brad Sugars has spoken on stage with the likes of Tom Hopkins, Brian Tracy, John Maxwell, Robert Kiyosaki, and Allen Pease, written books with people like Anthony Robbins, Jim Rohn, and Mark Victor Hansen, appeared on countless TV and radio programs and in literally hundreds of print articles around the globe. He's been voted as one of the Most Admired Entrepreneurs by the readers of *E-Spy* magazine—next to the likes of Rupert Murdoch, Henry Ford, Richard Branson, and Anita Roddick.

Today, *Action International* has coaches across the globe and is ranked as one of the Top 25 Fastest Growing Franchises on the planet as well as the #1 Business Consulting Franchise. The success of *Action International* is simply attributed to the fact that they apply the strategies their coaches use with business owners.

Brad is a proud father and husband, the chairman of a major childrens' charity, and in his own words, "a very average golfer."

Check out Brad's Web site www.bradsugars.com and read the literally hundreds of testimonials from those who've gone before you.

RECOMMENDED READING LIST

ACTION INTERNATIONAL BOOK LIST

"The only difference between *you* now and *you* in 5 years' time will be the people you meet and the books you read." Charlie Tremendous Jones

"And, the only difference between *your* income now and *your* income in 5 years' time will be the people you meet, the books you read, the tapes you listen to, and then how *you* apply it all." Brad Sugars

- *The E-Myth Revisited* by Michael E. Gerber
- *My Life in Advertising & Scientific Advertising* by Claude Hopkins
- *Tested Advertising Methods* by John Caples
- *Building the Happiness Centered Business* by Dr. Paddi Lund
- *Write Language* by Paul Dunn & Alan Pease
- *7 Habits of Highly Effective People* by Steven Covey
- *First Things First* by Steven Covey
- *Awaken the Giant Within* by Anthony Robbins
- *Unlimited Power* by Anthony Robbins
- *22 Immutable Laws of Marketing* by Al Ries & Jack Trout
- *21 Ways to Build a Referral Based Business* by Brad Sugars
- *21 Ways to Increase Your Advertising Response* by Mark Tier
- *The One Minute Salesperson* by Spencer Johnson & Larry Wilson
- *The One Minute Manager* by Spencer Johnson & Kenneth Blanchard
- *The Great Sales Book* by Jack Collis
- *Way of the Peaceful Warrior* by Dan Millman
- *How to Build a Championship Team*—Six Audio tapes by Blair Singer
- Brad Sugars "Introduction to Sales & Marketing" 3-hour Video
- Leverage—Board Game by Brad Sugars
- *17 Ways to Increase Your Business Profits* booklet & tape by Brad Sugars. FREE OF CHARGE to Business Owners

***To order Brad Sugars' products from the recommended reading list, call your nearest *Action International* office today.**

The 18 Most Asked Questions about Working with an *Action International* Business Coach

And 18 great reasons why you'll jump at the chance to get your business flying and make your dreams come true

1. So who is *Action International?*

Action International is a business Coaching and Consulting company started in 1993 by entrepreneur and author Brad Sugars. With offices around the globe and business coaches from Singapore to Sydney to San Francisco, *Action International* has been set up with you, the business owner, in mind.

Unlike traditional consulting firms, *Action* is designed to give you both short-term assistance and long-term training through its affordable Mentoring approach. After 12 years teaching business owners how to succeed, *Action's* more than 10,000 clients and 1,000,000 seminar attendees will attest to the power of the programs.

Based on the sales, marketing, and business management systems created by Brad Sugars, your *Action* Coach is trained to not only show you how to increase your business revenues and profits, but also how to develop the business so that you as the owner work less and relax more.

Action International is a franchised company, so your local *Action* Coach is a fellow business owner who's invested her own time, money, and energy to make her business succeed. At *Action,* your success truly does determine our success.

2. And, why do I need a Business Coach?

Every great sports star, business person, and superstar is surrounded by coaches and advisors.

And, as the world of business moves faster and gets more competitive, it's difficult to keep up with both the changes in your industry and the innovations in sales, marketing, and management strategies. Having a business coach is no longer a luxury; it's become a necessity.

On top of all that, it's impossible to get an objective answer from yourself. Don't get me wrong. You can survive in business without the help of a Coach, but it's almost impossible to thrive.

A Coach *can* see the forest for the trees. A Coach will make you focus on the game. A Coach will make you run more laps than you feel like. A Coach will tell it like it is. A Coach will give you small pointers. A Coach will listen. A Coach will be your marketing manager, your sales director, your training coordinator, your partner, your confidant, your mentor, your best friend, and an *Action* Business Coach will help you make your dreams come true.

3. Then, what's an Alignment Consultation?

Great question. It's where an *Action* Coach starts with every business owner. You'll invest a minimum of $1295, and during the initial 2 to 3 hours your Coach invests with you, he'll learn as much as he can about your business, your goals, your challenges, your sales, your marketing, your finances, and so much more.

All with three goals in mind: To know exactly where your business is now. To clarify your goals both in the business and personally. And thirdly, to get the crucial pieces of information he needs to create your businesses *Action* Plan for the next 12 months.

Not a traditional business or marketing plan mind you, but a step-by-step plan of *Action* that you'll work through as you continue with the Mentor Program.

4. So, what, then, is the Mentor Program?

Simply put, it's where your *Action* Coach will work with you for a full 12 months to make your goals a reality. From weekly coaching calls and goal-setting sessions, to creating marketing pieces together, you will develop new sales strategies and business systems so you can work less and learn all that you need to know about how to make your dreams come true.

You'll invest between $995 and $10,000 a month and your Coach will dedicate a minimum of 5 hours a month to working with you on your sales, marketing, team building, business development, and every step of the *Action* Plan you created from your Alignment Consultation.

Unlike most consultants, your *Action* Coach will do more than just show you what to do. She'll be with you when you need her most, as each idea takes shape, as each campaign is put into place, as you need the little pointers on making it happen, when you need someone to talk to, when you're faced with challenges and, most importantly, when you're just not sure what to do next. Your Coach will be there every step of the way.

5. Why at least 12 months?

If you've been in business for more than a few weeks, you've seen at least one or two so called "quick fixes."

Most Consultants seem to think they can solve all your problems in a few hours or a few days. At *Action* we believe that long-term success means not just scraping the surface and doing it for you. It means doing it with you, showing you how to do it, working alongside you, and creating the success together.

Over the 12 months, you'll work on different areas of your business, and month by month you'll not only see your goals become a reality, you'll gain both the confidence and the knowledge to make it happen again and again, even when your first 12 months of Coaching is over.

6. How can you be sure this will work in my industry and in my business?

Very simple. You see at *Action,* we're experts in the areas of sales, marketing, business development, business management, and team building just to name a few. With 328 different profit-building strategies, you'll soon see just how powerful these systems are.

You, on the other hand, are the expert in your business and together we can apply the *Action* systems to make your business fly.

Add to this the fact that within the *Action* Team at least one of our Coaches has either worked with, managed, worked in, or even owned a business that's the same or very similar to yours. Your *Action* Coach has the full resources of the entire *Action* team to call upon for every challenge you have. Imagine hundreds of experts ready to help you.

7. Won't this just mean more work?

Of course when you set the plan with your *Action* Coach, it'll all seem like a massive amount of work, but no one ever said attaining your goals would be easy.

In the first few months, it'll take some work to adjust, some work to get over the hump so to speak. The further you are into the program, the less and less work you'll have to do.

You will, however, be literally amazed at how focused you'll be and how much you'll get done. With focus, an *Action* Coach, and most importantly the *Action* Systems, you'll be achieving a whole lot more with the same or even less work.

8. How will I find the time?

Once again the first few months will be the toughest, not because of an extra amount of work, but because of the different work. In fact, your *Action* Coach will show you how to, on a day-to-day basis, get more work done with less effort.

In other words, after the first few months you'll find that you're not working more, just working differently. Then, depending on your goals from about month six onwards, you'll start to see the results of all your work, and if you choose to, you can start working less than ever before. Just remember, it's about changing what you do with your time, *not* putting in more time.

9. How much will I need to invest?

Nothing, if you look at it from the same perspective as we do. That's the difference between a cost and an investment. Everything you do with your *Action* Coach is a true investment in your future.

Not only will you create great results in your business, but you'll end up with both an entrepreneurial education second to none, and the knowledge that you can repeat your successes over and over again.

As mentioned, you'll need to invest at least $1295 up to $5000 for the Alignment Consultation and Training Day, and then between $995 and $10,000 a month for the next 12 months of coaching.

Your Coach may also suggest several books, tapes, and videos to assist in your training, and yes, they'll add to your investment as you go. Why? Because having an *Action* Coach is just like having a marketing manager, a sales team leader, a trainer, a recruitment specialist, and corporate consultant all for half the price of a secretary.

10. Will it cost me extra to implement the strategies?

Once again, give your *Action* Coach just half an hour and he'll show you how to turn your marketing into an investment that yields sales and profits rather than just running up your expenses.

In most cases we'll actually save you money when we find the areas that aren't working for you. But yes, I'm sure you'll need to spend some money to make some money.

Yet, when you follow our simple testing and measuring systems, you'll never risk more than a few dollars on each campaign, and when we find the ones that work, we make sure you keep profiting from them time and again.

Remember, when you go the accounting way of saving costs, you can only ever add a few percent to the bottom line.

Following Brad Sugars' formula, your *Action* Coach will show you that through sales, marketing, and income growth, your possible returns are exponential.

The sky's the limit, as they say.

11. Are there any guarantees?

To put it bluntly, no. Your *Action* Coach will never promise any specific results, nor will she guarantee that any of your goals will become a reality.

You see, we're your coach. You're still the player, and it's up to you to take the field. Your Coach will push you, cajole you, help you, be there for you, and even do some things with you, but you've still got to do the work.

Only *you* can ever be truly accountable for your own success and at *Action* we know this to be a fact. We guarantee to give you the best service we can, to answer your questions promptly, and with the best available information. And, last but not least your *Action* Coach is committed to making you successful whether you like it or not.

That's right, once we've set the goals and made the plan, we'll do whatever it takes to make sure you reach for that goal and strive with all your might to achieve all that you desire.

Of course we'll be sure to keep you as balanced in your life as we can. We'll make sure you never compromise either the long-term health and success of your company or yourself, and more importantly your personal set of values and what's important to you.

12. What results have other business owners seen?

Anything from previously working 60 hours a week down to working just 10—right through to increases in revenues of 100s and even 1000s of percent. Results speak for themselves. Be sure to keep reading for specific examples of real people, with real businesses, getting real results.

There are three reasons why this will work for you in your business. Firstly, your *Action* Coach will help you get 100 percent focused on your goals and the step-by-step processes to get you there. This focus alone is amazing in its effect on you and your business results.

Secondly, your coach will hold you accountable to get things done, not just for the day-to-day running of the business, but for the dynamic growth of the business. You're investing in your success and we're going to get you there.

Thirdly, your Coach is going to teach you one-on-one as many of *Action's* 328 profit-building strategies as you need. So whether your goal is to be making more money, or working fewer hours or both inside the next 12 months your goals can become a reality. Just ask any of the thousands of existing *Action* clients, or more specifically, check out the results of 19 of our most recent clients shown later in this section.

13. What areas will you coach me in?

There are five main areas your *Action* Coach will work on with you. Of course, how much of each depends on you, your business, and your goals.

Sales. The backbone of creating a superprofitable business, and one area we'll help you get spectacular results in.

Marketing and Advertising. If you want to get a sale, you've got to get a prospect. Over the next 12 months your *Action* Coach will teach you Brad Sugars' amazingly simple streetwise marketing—marketing that makes profits.

Team Building and Recruitment. You'll never *wish* for the right people again. You'll have motivated and passionate team members when your Coach shows you how.

Systems and Business Development. Stop the business from running you and start running your business. Your Coach will show you the secrets to having the business work, even when you're not there.

Customer Service. How to deliver consistently, make it easy to buy, and leave your customers feeling delighted with your service. Both referrals and repeat business are centered in the strategies your Coach will teach you.

14. Can you also train my people?

Yes. We believe that training your people is almost as important as coaching you.

Your investment starts at $1500 for your entire team, and you can decide between five very powerful in-house training programs. From "*Sales Made Simple*" for your face-to-face sales team to "*Phone Power*" for your entire team's telephone etiquette and sales ability. Then you can run the "*Raving Fans*" customer service training or the "*Total Team*" training. And finally, if you're too busy earning a living to make any real money, then you've just got to attend our "*Business Academy 101.*" It will make a huge impact on your finances, business, career, family, and lifestyle. You'll be amazed at how much involvement and excitement comes out of your team with each training program.

15. Can you write ads, letters, and marketing pieces for me?

Yes. Your *Action* Coach can do it for you, he can train you to do it yourself, or we can simply critique the marketing pieces you're using right now.

If you want us to do it for you, our one-time fees start at just $1195. You'll not only get one piece; we'll design several pieces for you to take to the market and see which one performs the best. Then, if it's a critique you're after, just $349 means we'll work through your entire piece and give you feedback on what to change, how to change it, and what else you should do. Last but not least, for between $15 and $795 we can recommend a variety of books, tapes, and most importantly, Brad Sugars' Instant Success series books that'll take you step-by-step through the how-tos of creating your marketing pieces.

16. Why do you also recommend books, tapes, and videos?

Basically, to save you time and money. Take Brad Sugars' *Sales Rich* DVD or Video Series, for instance. In about 16 hours you'll learn more about business than you have in the last 12 years. It'll also mean your *Action* Coach works with you on the high-level implementation rather than the very basic teaching.

It's a very powerful way for you to speed up the coaching process and get phenomenal rather than just great results.

17. When is the best time to get started?

Yesterday. OK, seriously, right now, today, this minute, before you take another step, waste another dollar, lose another sale, work too many more hours, miss another family event, forget another special occasion.

Far too many business people wait and see. They think working harder will make it all better. Remember, what you know got you to where you are. To get to where you want to go, you've got to make some changes and most probably learn something new.

There's no time like the present to get started on your dreams and goals.

18. So how do we get started?

Well, you'd better get back in touch with your *Action* Coach. There's some very simple paperwork to sign, and then you're on your way.

You'll have to invest a few hours showing them everything about your business. Together you'll get a plan created and then the work starts. Remember, it may seem like a big job at the start, but with a Coach, you're sharing the load and together you'll achieve great things.

Here's what others say about what happened after working with an *Action* business coach

Paul and Rosemary Rose—Icontact Multimedia

"Our *Action* coach showed us several ways to help market our product. We went on to triple our client base and simultaneously tripled our profits in just seven months. It was unbelievable! Last year was our best Christmas ever. We were really able to spoil ourselves!"

S. Ford—Pride Kitchens

"In 6 months, I've gone from working more than 60 hours per week in my business to less than 20, and my conversion rate's up from 19 percent to 62 percent. I've now got some life back!"

Gary and Leanne Paper—Galea Timber Products

"We achieved our goal for the 12 months within a 6-month period with a 100 percent increase in turnover and a good increase in margins. We have already recommended and will continue to recommend this program to others."

Russell, Kevin, John, and Karen—Northern Lights Power and Distribution

"Our profit margin has increased from 8 percent to 21 percent in the last 8 months. *Action* coaching focussed us on what are our most profitable markets."

Ty Pedersen—De Vries Marketing Sydney

"After just three months of coaching, my sales team's conversion rate has grown from an average of less than 12 percent to more than 23 percent and our profits have climbed by more than 30 percent."

Hank Meerkerk and Hemi McGarvey—B.O.P. School of Welding

"Last year we started off with a profit forecast, but as soon as we got *Action* involved we decided to double our forecast. We're already well over that forecast again by two-and-a-half times on turnover, and profits are even higher. Now we run a really profitable business."

Stuart Birch—Education Personnel Limited

"One direct mail letter added $40,000 to my bottom line, and working with *Action* has given me quality time to work on my business and spend time with my family."

Mark West—Wests Pumping and Irrigation

"In four months two simple strategies have increased our business more than 20 percent. We're so busy, we've had to delay expanding the business while we catch up!"

Michael Griffiths—Gym Owner

"I went from working 70 hours per week *in* the business to just 25 hours, with the rest of the time spent working *on* the business."

Cheryl Standring—In Harmony Landscapes

"We tried our own direct mail and only got a 1 percent response. With *Action* our response rate increased to 20 percent. It's definitely worth every dollar we've invested."

Jason and Chris Houston—Empradoor Finishing

"After 11 months of working with *Action,* we have increased our sales by 497 percent, and the team is working without our having to be there."

Michael Avery—Coomera Pet Motels

"I was skeptical at first, but I knew we needed major changes in our business. In 2 months, our extra profits were easily covering our investment and our predictions for the next 10 months are amazing."

Garry Norris—North Tax & Accounting

"As an accountant, my training enables me to help other business people make more money. It is therefore refreshing when someone else can help me do the same. I have a policy of only referring my clients to people who are professional, good at what they do, and who have personally given me great service. *Action* fits all three of these criteria, and I recommend *Action* to my business clients who want to grow and develop their businesses further."

Lisa Davis and Steve Groves—Mt. Eden Motorcycles

"With *Action* we increased our database from 800 to 1200 in 3 months. We consistently get about 20 new qualified people on our database each week for less than $10 per week."

Christine Pryor—U-Name-It Embroidery

"Sales for August this year have increased 352 percent. We're now targeting a different market and we're a lot more confident about what we're doing."

Joseph Saitta and Michelle Fisher—Banyule Electrics

"Working with *Action,* our inquiry rate has doubled. In four months our business has changed so much our customers love us. It's a better place for people to work and our margins are widening."

Kevin and Alison Snook—Property Sales

"In the 12 months previous to working with *Action,* we had sold one home in our subdivision. In the first eight months of working with *Action,* we sold six homes. The results speak for themselves."

Wayne Manson—Hospital Supplies

"When I first looked at the Mentoring Program it looked expensive, but from the inside looking out, its been the best money I have ever spent. Sales are up more than $3000 per month since I started, and the things I have learned and expect to learn will ensure that I will enjoy strong sustainable growth in the future."

Action Contact Details

***Action International* Asia Pacific**

Ground Floor, *Action* House, 2 Mayneview Street, Milton QLD 4064

Ph: +61 (0) 7 3368 2525

Fax: +61 (0) 7 3368 2535

Free Call: 1800 670 335

***Action International* Europe**

Olympic House, Harbor Road, Howth, Co. Dublin, Ireland

Ph: +353 (0) 1-8320213

Fax: +353 (0) 1-8394934

***Action International* North America**

5670 Wynn Road Suite A & C, Las Vegas, Nevada 89118

Ph: +1 (702) 795 3188

Fax: +1 (702) 795 3183

Free Call: (888) 483 2828

***Action International* UK**

3-5 Richmond Hill, Richmond, Surrey, TW 106RE

Ph: +44 020 8948 5151

Fax: +44 020 8948 4111

Action Offices around the globe:

Australia | Canada | China | England | France | Germany | Hong Kong

India | Indonesia | Ireland | Malaysia | Mexico | New Zealand

Phillippines | Scotland | Spain | Singapore | USA | Wales

Here's how you can profit from all of Brad's ideas with your local *Action* *International* Business Coach

Just like a sporting coach pushes an athlete to achieve optimum performance, provides them with support when they are exhausted, and teaches the athlete to execute plays that the competition does not anticipate.

A business coach will make you run more laps than you feel like. A business coach will show it like it is. And a business coach will listen.

The role of an ***Action*** Business Coach is to show you how to improve your business through guidance, support, and encouragement. Your coach will help you with your sales, marketing, management, team building, and so much more. Just like a sporting coach, your ***Action*** Business Coach will help you and your business perform at levels you never thought possible.

Whether you've been in business for a week or 20 years, it's the right time to meet with and see how you'll profit from an ***Action*** Coach.

As the owner of a business it's hard enough to keep pace with all the changes and innovations going on in your industry, let alone to find the time to devote to sales, marketing, systems, planning and team management, and then to run your business as well.

As the world of business moves faster and becomes more competitive, having a Business Coach is no longer a luxury; it has become a necessity. Based on the sales, marketing, and business management systems created by Brad Sugars, your ***Action*** Coach is trained to not only show you how to increase your business revenues and profits but also how to develop your business so that you, as the owner, can take back control. All with the aim of your working less and relaxing more. Making money is one thing; having the time to enjoy it is another.

Your ***Action*** Business Coach will become your marketing manager, your sales director, your training coordinator, your confidant, your mentor. In short, your ***Action*** Coach will help you make your business dreams come true.

ATTENTION BUSINESS OWNERS
You can increase your profits now

Here's how you can have one of Brad's ***Action*** *International* Business Coaches guide you to success.

Like every successful sporting icon or team, a business needs a coach to help it achieve its full potential. In order to guarantee your business success, you can have one of Brad's team as your business coach. You will learn about how you can get amazing results with the help of the team at ***Action*** *International.*

The business coaches are ready to take you and your business on a journey that will reward you for the rest of your life. You see, we believe ***Action*** speaks louder than words.

Complete and post this card to your local ***Action*** office to discover how our team can help you increase your income today!

Action *International*

The World's Number-1 Business Coaching Team

Name ....

Position ....

Company ....

Address ....

....

Country ....

Phone ....

Fax ....

Email ....

Referred by ....

How do I become an *Action International* Business Coach?

If you choose to invest your time and money in a great business and you're looking for a white-collar franchise opportunity to build yourself a lifestyle, an income, a way to take control of your life and, a way to get great personal satisfaction ...

Then you've just found the world's best team!

Now, it's about finding out if you've got what it takes to really enjoy and thrive in this amazing business opportunity.

Here are the 4 things we look for in every *Action* Coach:

1. You've got to love succeeding

We're looking for people who love success, who love getting out there and making things happen. People who enjoy mixing with other people, people who thrive on learning and growing, and people who want to charge an hourly rate most professionals only dream of.

2. You've got to love being in charge of your own life

When you're ready to take control, the key is to be in business for yourself, but not by yourself. ***Action***'s support, our training, our world leading systems, and the backup of a global team are all waiting to give you the best chance of being an amazing business success.

3. You've got to love helping people

Being a great Coach is all about helping yourself by helping others. The first time clients thank you for showing them step by step how to make more money and work less within their business, will be the day you realize just how great being an ***Action*** Business Coach really is.

4. You've got to love a great lifestyle

Working from home, setting your own timetable, spending time with family and friends, knowing that the hard work you do is for your own company and, not having to climb a so-called corporate ladder. This is what lifestyle is all about. Remember, business is supposed to give you a life, not take it away.

Our business is booming and we're seriously looking for people ready to find out more about how becoming a member of the ***Action*** *International* Business Coaching team is going to be the best decision you've ever made.

Apply online now at www.action-international.com

Here's how you can network, get new leads, build yourself an instant sales team, learn, grow and build a great team of supportive business owners around you by checking into your local *Action* Profit Club

Joining your local *Action* Profit Club is about more than just networking, it's also the learning and exchanging of profitable ideas.

Embark on a journey to a more profitable enterprise by meeting with fellow, like-minded business owners.

An ***Action*** Profit Club is an excellent way to network with business people and business owners. You will meet every two weeks for breakfast to network and learn profitable strategies to grow your business.

Here are three reasons why ***Action*** *International's* Profit Clubs work where other networking groups don't:

1. You know networking is a great idea. The challenge is finding the time and maintaining the motivation to keep it up and make it a part of your business. If you're not really having fun and getting the benefits, you'll find it gets easier to find excuses that stop you going. So, we guarantee you will always have fun and learn a lot from your bi-weekly group meetings.
2. The real problem is that so few people do any work 'on' their business. Instead they generally work "in" it, until it's too late. By being a member of an ***Action*** Profit Club, you get to attend FREE business-building workshops run by Business Coaches that teach you how to work "on" your business and avoid this common pitfall and help you to grow your business.
3. Unlike other groups, we have marketing systems to assist in your groups' growth rather than just relying on you to bring in new members. This way you can concentrate on YOUR business rather than on ours.

Latest statistics show that the average person knows at least 200 other contacts. By being a member of your local ***Action*** Profit Club, you have an instant network of around 3,000 people

Join your local *Action* Profit Club today.

Apply online now at www.actionprofitclub.com

LEVERAGE—The Game of Business
Your Business Success is just a Few Games Away

Leverage—The Game of Business is a fun way to learn how to succeed in business fast.

The rewards start flowing the moment you start playing!

Leverage is three hours of fun, learning, and discovering how you can be an amazingly successful business person.

It's a breakthrough in education that will have you racking up the profits in no time. The principles you take away from playing this game will set you up for a life of business success. It will open your mind to what's truly possible. Apply what you learn and **sit back and watch your profits soar.**

By playing this fun and interactive business game, you will learn:

- How to quickly raise your business income
- How business people can become rich and successful in a short space of time
- How to create a business that works without you

Isn't it time you had the edge over your competition?

Leverage has been played by all age groups from 12-85 and has been a huge learning experience for all. The most common comment we hear is: 'I thought I knew a lot, and just by playing a simple board game I have realized I have a long way to go. The knowledge I've gained from playing Leverage will make me thousands! Thanks for the lesson.'

To order your copy online today, please visit www.bradsugars.com